美點佳餚2
簡易點心

歐陽紉詩編著

Chopsticks Recipes
Dim Sum
by Mrs. Cecilia J. Au Yeung

D0925488

嘉饌家政中心出版
Publisher: Chopsticks Cooking Centre

Published and Distributed by
Publication Department
Chopsticks Cooking Centre
Kowloon Central P.O. Box 3515, HONG KONG
122 Waterloo Road, 3rd Floor, Kowloon, HONG KONG
Tel: 3-015989, 3-015911
© Cecilia J. AU-YEUNG
1st print   June 1976
2nd print April 1978
3rd print February 1979

Printed by Yu Luen Offset Printing Factory Ltd.

Price: HK$12.00
ISBN 962 7018 02 3

出版者及總批發
嘉饌家政中心　出版部

香港　九龍中央郵箱３５１５號
香港　九龍窩打老道１２２號四樓
電話：3－015989　3－015911
每册售價港

INTRODUCTION

Dear readers,

     I am a registered D.S. teacher with 20 years experience in the cooking field. I would now like to share the knowledge about Chinese Cooking which I had learnt from the past with you. This edition of "Dim Sum" not only contains 52 recipes of making famous Chinese snacks, it also informs you of specific terms used in cookery, introduces Chinese cooking utensils, helps you to verify different cereals and to differentiate among various kinds of flour. I hope that this cookbook would be a useful guide to better methods of cooking.

     Besides publishing cookbooks, I also teach cooking in Chopsticks Cooking Centre. I am more than happy if you are interested in cooking and would join us in learning. There are classes for the convenience of different people with different occupations, and there are courses for learning different kinds of cooking. It depends on individual requirements and needs to decide which course to take and which class to fit in. Based on the idea of assisting children from ages 6 to 12 to develop a healthy hobby and training them to become responsible and skilful as they grow up, a Children Class was started last year, teaching children to make simple food.

     So, why don't you let your children join us in their leisure time, or during vacations?

Cecilia J. Au-Yeung (Mrs.)
Principal

目錄　CONTENTS

糕: 豬油馬拉糕　Vanilla Sponge _____ 6

蔗糖蒸年糕　Chinese New Year Pudding _____ 8

西施蒸蛋糕　Steamed Sponge _____ 10

衛生紅豆糕　Red Bean Pudding _____ 12

清涼蔗汁糕　Sugar Cane pudding _____ 14

腊味蘿白糕　Turnip Pudding _____ 16

角: 叉燒魚皮角　Fish Triangle in Soup _____ 18

鬆軟咸水角　Deep Fried Savoury Triangle _____ 20

香炸荔芋角　Deep Fried Taro Pasty _____ 22

餅: 嘉饌炸酥餅　Chopsticks Crisp _____ 24

棗蓉金露酥　Date Jam Crisp _____ 26

椰蓉炸酥盒　Flaky Coconut Patty _____ 28

五彩皮蛋酥　Thousand Years Egg Crisp _____ 30

酥脆合桃酥　Walnut Crisp _____ 32

叉燒焗酥餅　Cha Shiu Crisp _____ 34

千層老婆餅　Winter Melon Crisp _____ 36

蝦米沙葛餅　Carrot Cake _____ 38

香脆葱油餅　Green Onion Coil _____ 40

家鄉煎薄餅　Chinese Savoury Pancake _____ 42

香甜水晶餅　Crystal Cake _____ 44

荔芋肉茸餅　Taro Croquette _____ 46

脆皮鮮蝦盒　Crispy Meat Pie _____ 48

豬油炒米餅　Rice Flour Cookie _____ 50

飽: 生煎菜肉飽　Vegetable Meat Pie _____ 52

酥皮蓮蓉飽　Sweet Paste Bun _____ 54

蠔油叉燒飽　Cha Shiu Bun _____ 56

肉餡小籠飽　Steamed Meat Bun _____ 58

卷：	什錦糯米卷	Glutinous Rice Roll	60
	省時臘腸卷	Chinese Sausage Roll	62
	蛋煎班戟卷	Savoury Pancake Roll	64
	三絲炸春卷	Spring Roll	66
	三絲蒸粉卷	Rice Flour Sheet Roll	68
布甸：	牛油焗布甸	Butter Pudding	70
	焗西米布甸	Sago Pudding	72
粽：	蛋黃豆沙粽	Red Bean Paste Dumpling	74
	加料裹蒸粽	Luxurious Rice Dumpling	76
	脆皮油炸粽	Rice Dumpling Fritter	78
	錦繡糯米雞	Steamed Rice Dumpling with Assorted Meat	80
糍：	椰蓉糯米糍	Coconut Snow Ball	82
	豆沙煎軟糍	Sweet Paste Cookies	84
其他：	香滑紅豆沙	Red Bean Paste Filling	86
	賀歲蛋散仔	New Year Cruller	88
	脆炸馬蹄條	Water Chestnut Fritter	90
	酸甜炸雲吞	Sweet and Sour Won Ton	92
	芝蔴薯茸棗	Sweet Potato Croquette	94
	雞絲銀針粉	Silver Pin Noodle with Shredded Chicken	96
	百花芝蔴蝦	Sesame Prawn Triangle	98
	鮮肉餡湯丸	Glutinous Rice Balls in Soup	100
	乾蒸豬肉賣	Shiu My	102
	山竹蒸牛肉	Steamed Minced Beef Ball	104
	鬆化椰絲堆	Deep Fried Sesame Ball	106
	上湯蝦肉餃	Shrimp Dumplings in Soup	108

豬油馬拉糕

材料：麵粉8安　　　　吉士粉2安
　　　發粉2茶匙　　　梳打粉½茶匙
　　　鷄蛋6隻　　　　糖12安
　　　豬油5安　　　　欖仁20粒
　　　雲呢喇香油½茶匙

製法：①將麵粉、吉士粉、發粉、梳打
　　　　粉同篩兩次候用。
　　　②鷄蛋打開放在大盆中，用打蛋
　　　　器打爛、逐漸加入砂糖同打至
　　　　輕軟。
　　　③將已篩過兩次之混合粉料篩入
　　　　蛋液中、加香油以蛋拂輕輕覆
　　　　入撈勻，放置一旁約三十分鐘。
　　　④豬油坐在溫水中熱成流質，慢
　　　　慢加入拌勻。
　　　⑤蒸籠內放一不銹鋼方格，剪兩
　　　　張長方白紙對放在方格內，紙
　　　　上塗油，將粉料倒入，猛火蒸
　　　　約五十分鐘，欖仁放在羔面作
　　　　裝飾用。

Vanilla Sponge

INGREDIENTS:

8 oz. flour
2 oz. custard powder
2 tsp. baking powder
½ tsp. bicarbonate soda
½ tsp. vanilla essence
6 eggs
12 oz. sugar
5 oz. lard
20 olive kernels

METHOD:

1. Sift flour, custard powder, baking powder, and bicarbonate soda together twice, then leave aside.
2. Beat eggs in a bowl, add in sugar gradually and continue beating until mixture is light and fluffy.
3. Sift dry ingredients and fold into the egg-mixture. Add vanilla essence. Leave aside for 30 minutes.
4. Heat lard into a fluid form. Gradually add into the batter.
5. Line two pieces of greased paper in a square, then put into steamer. Pour batter in and steam for about 50 minutes. Arrange olive kernels for decoration.

蔗糖蒸年糕

材料： 糯米粉２８安　　　汀麵１６安
蔗糖３磅　　　　　水６杯
豬油３湯匙　　　　硼砂１茶匙

製法： ①糯米粉與汀麵混合一同篩在大
　　　盆中。
②鍋中放水６杯，置中火爐上加
　　　蔗糖煮沸。糖完全溶化後加入
　　　豬油及硼砂搞勻。
③將已搞勻之糖水用密篩隔住冲
　　　進混合粉料中，用木棍搞拌，
　　　邊冲邊搞。
④羔盆塗油，將混合料再以篩隔
　　　住倒入盆中。如發現有粉粒，
　　　可以手搓爛流入盆中。
⑤鑊中放水大半鍋，架上一格蒸
　　　籠　羔盆放在另一隔蒸籠內，
　　　待水大滾時，即將放置羔盆之
　　　蒸籠架在鑊中之蒸籠上，中火
　　　蒸約二小時，攤凍後可切片食
　　　，亦可沾蛋液稍煎。

Chinese New Year Pudding

INGREDIENTS:

28 oz. glutinous rice flour
16 oz. wheat starch
3 lb. brown sugar
6 cups water
3 tbsp. lard
1 tsp. borax

METHOD:

1. Sift glutinous rice flour and wheat starch into a mixing bowl.
2. Boil 6 cups water with brown sugar. When sugar has dissolved, add lard and borax.
3. Using a seive, pour liquid into flour. Stir while adding in liquid.
4. Pour fluid mixture into a greased tin through a seive again.
5. Fill the wok with a lot of water and bring to boil. Put a steamer over boiling water. Place the pudding tin in another steamer and add to the top of the previous one. Steam pudding over medium.heat for 2 hours. Let cool and serve. Can.also be dipped in beaten eggs and fried.

REMARKS: This New Year Pudding can be kept for 2 months.

西施蒸蛋糕

材料：鷄蛋9隻　　　　白糖１２安
　　　　麵粉１０安　　　芫茜２棵
　　　　咸蛋王２隻

製法：①鷄蛋逐隻打入蛋羔桶中。
　　　　②糖逐少加入蛋羔桶中，以打蛋
　　　　　器打之，一直打到鷄蛋鬆軟浮
　　　　　起。
　　　　③將麵粉用篩輕輕篩入蛋液中，
　　　　　分數次撈勻。
　　　　④羔盆或蛋羔杯中塗油，將混合
　　　　　物倒至八分滿，放入猛火滾住
　　　　　之蒸籠內蒸半小時。
　　　　⑤芫茜葉及咸蛋王於未蒸前排放
　　　　　在蛋羔面上作裝飾用。

Steamed Sponge

INGREDIENTS:

9 eggs
12 oz. sugar
10 oz. flour
2 sprigs Chinese parsley
2 preserved egg yolks

METHOD:

1. Beat eggs in a mixing bowl one at a time.
2. Add in sugar gradually and whisk until fluffy.
3. Sift flour and fold into egg mixture with a metal spoon.
4. Turn mixture into greased cake tin not more than ¾ full. Allow room for rising. Decorate with Chinese parsley and chopped egg yolks.
5. Put tin into steamer over high heat for half an hour.

衛生紅豆糕

材料： 紅豆１磅　　　　　水８杯
冰糖１８安　　　　豬油½杯
粘米粉１４安加水３杯和勻

製法： ①紅豆揀淨後以水洗過、隔清水
份。
②將８杯水倒在深鍋內，加入紅
豆用中火煮沸。轉用慢火焙至
開花、約需一小時。
③加入冰糖同煮至糖溶後，倒入
豬油拌勻。
④粘米粉篩在大盆中，將３杯水
倒入開成粉漿。然後把粉漿慢
慢流入紅豆沙中搞勻。
⑤羔盆塗油，將混合物倒入撥平
。轉放猛火蒸籠內蒸一小時。
取出攤凍切片。

Red Bean Pudding

INGREDIENTS:

1 lb. red beans
8 cups water
18 oz. rock sugar
½ cup lard
14 oz. rice flour mixed with 3 cups water

METHOD:

1. Wash red beans and drain.
2. Pour 8 cups water into deep saucepan, add in red beans and bring to boil over medium heat. Lower the heat to simmer for about 1 hour until beans are tender.
3. Add in rock sugar to cook until melted. Pour in lard and stir well.
4. Sift rice flour into mixing bowl, mix into batter with 3 cups water. Stir batter in the bean mixture gradually until well blended.
5. Pour mixture into greased cake tin, steam in steamer over high heat for 1 hour. Serve in pieces.

清涼蔗汁糕

材料：馬蹄粉１０安　　　蔗汁６杯
　　　　水２杯　　　　　　糖８安
　　　　豬油２安

製法：①馬蹄粉倒入大盆中，加入蔗汁
　　　　２杯和勻、用密篩隔去雜質。
　　　②深鍋一隻，將水及蔗汁倒入，
　　　　加糖用文火煮沸、跟着加入豬
　　　　油。
　　　③糖完全溶後，慢慢倒入馬蹄粉
　　　　水。邊倒邊搞、至粉水加完，
　　　　再滾即可收火。
　　　④羔盆塗油，將混合料倒入盆內
　　　　，置猛火蒸籠內蒸約四十分鐘
　　　　，取出攤凍。放入雪柜過夜即
　　　　可。

Sugar Cane Pudding

INGREDIENTS:

10 oz. water chestnut powder
6 cups sugar cane juice
2 cups water
8 oz. sugar
2 oz. lard

METHOD:

1. Put water chestnut powder in a bowl, mix well with 2 cups of sugar cane juice.
2. Pour 2 cups water in a deep saucepan. Put in sugar and 4 cups of sugar cane juice then bring to the boil. Add lard and mix well.
3. Slowly stir water chestnut mixture into saucepan.
4. Pour the fluid mixture in a greased tin and steam for about 40 minutes over high heat. Let cool and put in refrigerator. Serve cold.

腊味蘿蔔糕

材料： 蝦米3安　　　　腊肉6安
　　　　腊腸4條　　　　冬菇半安
　　　　葱頭一粒　　　　蘿蔔4磅
　　　　粘米粉10安　　　（除皮）

調味： 鹽1½湯匙　　　　糖2湯匙
　　　　鷄精一粒　　　　古月粉半茶匙
　　　　青葱3條切粒
　　　　豬油或生油大半杯

製法： ①蝦米、冬菇用水洗淨浸透。將
　　　　蝦米剁成茸、冬菇蒸熟切粒、
　　　　腊肉腊腸以熱水洗淨切粒。
　　　②燒紅鑊，加油炸香葱頭棄去。
　　　　倒入蝦米爆香，加入腊味粒兜
　　　　炒片刻，將冬菇粒放下同炒。
　　　　盛起待用。
　　　③蘿蔔去皮洗淨刨成幼絲、倒下
　　　　燒紅之鑊中，加油同煮，邊煮
　　　　邊以鑊鏟不時翻動，煮至蘿蔔
　　　　完全變色時，加入腊味粒搞拌。
　　　④粘米粉篩於鑊中之混合物內，

以鑊兜勻、加調味品試味。
⑤羔盆塗油，倒入混合物扒平，
　置猛火蒸籠內蒸二小時。
⑥取出用塗油匙羮燙平羔面，洒
　上青葱粒。

註： 此糕只用蘿蔔本身之
　　水份，毋須另加水。

Turnip Pudding

INGREDIENTS:

3 oz. dried shrimp
6 oz. preserved pork
4 Chinese preserved sausage
½ oz. dried mushroom
1 shallot
4 lb. turnip (peeled)
10 oz. rice flour

SEASONINGS:

1½ tbsp. salt
1½ tbsp. sugar
1 concentrated chicken cube
½ tsp. pepper
3 green onions
¾ cup lard or oil

METHOD:

1. Wash and soak dried shrimps and mushrooms. Mash shrimps, steam and dice mushrooms. Wash preserved pork and Chinese sausages in warm water and dice.
2. Heat oil in a wok, saute shallot and discard. Put in mashed dried shrimps to fry, then add in diced preserved meat. Finally add mushrooms and saute for a while. Dish all cooked ingredients for further use.
3. Peel and shred turnip. Pour shredded turnip into a very hot wok. Add oil and stir from time to time while boiling. Cook until turnip changes colour. Add in preserved meat and mix well.
4. Sift rice flour into the mixture in wok, add in seasonings and blend together.
5. Oil cake tin, pour in mixture and flatten the top. Put in a large steamer and steam over high heat for 2 hours.
6. Remove turnip pudding from steamer after 2 hours and flatten the top with an oiled spoon. Sprinkle chopped green onion on top.

REMARKS: Shredded cabbage can be used in place of turnip.

叉燒魚皮角

材料： 皮—鮫魚肉10安
　　　　生粉２安

　　　　餡—叉燒６安　　　菜甫１安
　　　　　　冬菇２隻　　　甘笋１安
　　　　　　蔥２條

調味： 鹽½茶匙　　　　糖½茶匙
　　　　生抽１茶匙　　　古月粉少許
　　　　麻油少許　　　　生粉½茶匙

製法： ①將鮫魚肉以刀刮出，放在深盆
　　　　中加入生粉２安、調味品中之
　　　　一半鹽、糖古月粉攪成膠狀。
　　　　②叉燒切指甲片、菜甫甘笋飛水
　　　　後切指甲片、冬菇蒸熟切幼粒
　　　　、蔥切幼粒。
　　　　③燒紅鑊加油爆香各粒，加調味
　　　　品炒透以生粉水打獻兜勻、洒
　　　　下蔥粒。
　　　　④取出魚膠，用生粉作焙以手捏
　　　　成扁圓形、將餡放入對角覆起

捏成角形。放入沸水中煮至浮
起、撈起過冷水。
⑤鍋中置上湯４杯煮沸後加油、
放入菜遠滾片刻，加入魚皮角
再滾即成。

Fish Triangle in Soup

INGREDIENTS:

PASTRY—

10 oz. minced fish
2 oz. corn flour

FILLING—

6 oz. cha shiu
1 oz. preserved turnip
1 oz. carrot
2 dried mushrooms
2 green onions

SEASONINGS:

½ tsp. salt
½ tsp. sugar
1 tsp. light soy
½ tsp. corn flour
little sesame oil
dash of pepper

METHOD:

1. Scrape flesh from mackerel into deep bowl, discard skin. Add in 2 oz. corn starch, half of the seasonings and pound until firm.
2. Wash and dice preserved turnip and cha shiu. Boil and dice carrot. Steam and dice mushroom. Chop green onion.
3. Heat a pan with oil and saute diced ingredients. Add in seasonings and fry, use corn starch and water solution to make gravy. Sprinkle with chopped green onion.
4. Take out fish pastry, use little at a time, sprinkle on starch and knead into a flat round with hands. Wrap in filling, fold pastry in halves and seal the edge. Put into boiling water to boil until triangles float, drain and blanch with cold water.
5. Pour 4 cups stock in saucepan, add in any kind of oil when boiled. Put in green vegetable, continue to boil for a while, add fish triangles in soup and bring to boil again. Serve hot.

鬆軟咸水角

材料： 皮—汀麵2安　　　沸水2安
　　　　糯米粉8安　　　凍水⅔杯
　　　　糖2安　　　　　豬油2安

　　　　餡—豬肉6安　　　蝦米2安
　　　　菜甫2安　　　　甘笋2安
　　　　冬菇1隻　　　　葱粒1湯匙

調味： 香鹽½茶匙　　　　糖1茶匙
　　　　酒1茶匙　　　　　古月粉少許
　　　　蔴油少許　　　　　生粉½茶匙

製法： ①汀麵篩在大盆中，將沸水沖入
　　　　、用木棍搞勻。
　　　　②糯米粉篩於桌上，加入凍水搓
　　　　匀。再加汀麵團及糖一同搓至
　　　　軟滑。
　　　　③將粉團分成3份，放兩份於蒸
　　　　籠內蒸十分鐘。取出與其餘三
　　　　份一生粉團及豬油一同搓滑。
　　　　④豬肉切幼粒以少許調味料醃十
　　　　分鐘，泡油候用。

⑤蝦米、冬菇洗淨浸透切成幼粒
。菜甫、甘笋飛水後亦切成幼
粒。

⑥燒紅鑊加油、將蝦米冬菇爆香
，加入其他各幼粒兜炒片刻、
贊酒調味再炒、以生粉水打獻
加葱粒兜勻。

⑦將粉團搓成長條，平均分為卅
二件、以手揑薄邊沿，放入餡
料收口弄成角形，放入中火油
鑊中炸至金黃色。

Deep Fried Savoury Triangle

INGREDIENTS:

PASTRY—

2 oz. wheat starch
2 oz. boiling water
8 oz. glutinous rice flour
¾ cup cold water
2 oz. sugar
2 oz. lard

FILLING—

6 oz. pork
2 oz. dried shrimp
2 oz. preserved turnip
2 oz. carrot
1 dried mushroom
1 tbsp. chopped green onion

SEASONINGS:

½ tsp. spicy salt
1 tsp. sugar
1 tsp. wine
dash of pepper
dash of sesame oil
½ tsp. corn starch

METHOD:

1. Sift wheat starch in a bowl, pour in 2 oz. boiling water, stir immediately.
2. Sift glutinous rice flour on table, add water and mix well. Knead wheat starch dough with glutinous rice flour dough and sugar till soft.
3. Divide dough into 3 portions then steam 2 portions for 10 minutes. Take out and knead the 3 portions together till smooth. Leave for further use.
4. Wash dried shrimps and soak well. Chop.
5. Wash and dice preserved turnip, pork and carrot.
6. Heat a pan, add a little oil and saute all ingredients. Sprinkle a little wine, then season well. Add in corn starch solution to make gravy.
7. Roll and cut the dough into 32 equal parts. Press into rounds and put in filling. Fold and seal edges together securely. Deep fry in hot oil until golden brown.

REMARKS: Spicy salt is made from mixing 1 lb. fine salt with 1 oz. mix spice.

香炸荔芋角

材料： 皮—荔甫芋２０安　　汀麵３安
　　　　沸水３安　　　　　豬油６安
　　　　鹽一茶匙　　　　　糖２安
　　　　乾汀麵一安作焙

　　　　餡料—枚肉６安　　　蝦肉６安
　　　　冬菇３隻　　　　　笋肉２安
　　　　雞蛋１隻

調味： 鹽⅓茶匙　　　　　糖半茶匙
　　　　雞精⅓粒　　　　　生抽一茶匙
　　　　古月粉及麻油少許　生粉一茶匙

製法： ①芋頭刨皮洗淨，切成６大件。
　　　　　置蒸籠內蒸熟後，取出淨肉二
　　　　　十安候用。
　　　　②汀麵放大盆中，加沸水冲入搞
　　　　　勻，與芋頭同放肉搞中搞爛。
　　　　③將搞爛之混合物放在桌上搓勻
　　　　　。邊搓邊加豬油。然後撥開一
　　　　　穴放入鹽糖用力同搓至軟滑。
　　　　　搓成長條切成廿四等份。

④枚肉、蝦肉切粒、冬菇浸透蒸
　熟切粒，笋飛水後亦切粒。
⑤枚肉用一部份調味品醃十分鐘
　，蝦肉以生粉、鹽撈過泡嫩油
　、枚肉亦泡油候用。
⑥燒紅鑊、將冬菇冬笋放入爆炒
　片刻，加入肉類贊酒調味打獻
　後，撈入雞蛋拌勻盛起。
⑦將每份皮料包入餡料一份，挹
　好後放在中火油鑊中炸至鬆皮
　。

Deep Fried Taro Pasty

INGREDIENTS:

PASTRY—

20 oz. taro
3 oz. wheat starch
3 oz. boiling water
6 oz. lard
1 tsp. salt
2 oz. sugar
a little wheat starch for dusting

FILLING—

6 oz. lean pork
6 oz. shelled shrimp
3 dried mushrooms
2 oz. bamboo shoot or carrot
1 egg

SEASONINGS:

¾ tsp. salt
½ tsp. sugar
¼ chicken cube
1 tsp. light soy
dash of sesame oil
dash of pepper
1 tsp. corn starch

METHOD:

1. Peel and wash taro, cut into 6 pieces. Steam in steamer and sort out 20 oz. for further use.
2. Use wheat starch in a mixing bowl, add in boiling water and stir well. Put into mincer together with taro and mince.
3. Sprinkle a little wheat starch on table, put on minced mixture and knead. Meanwhile add in salt and sugar, continue to knead into a smooth dough. Make a long roll and divide into 24 equal parts.
4. Dice lean pork and shelled shrimps. Soak, steam and dice mushrooms. Boil and dice bamboo shoots.
5. Marinade lean pork with part of the seasonings for 10 minutes. Mix shrimps with corn starch and salt. Saute shrimps and pork for further use.
6. Saute mushrooms and bamboo shoot in a hot pan for a while and fry assorted meat with wine and seasonings. Add in beaten egg to mix together as filling.
7. Wrap filling in each portion of pastry. Draw edges to seal and deep fry in warm oil until pastry become flaky.

REMARKS: Taro can be substituted by potatoes.

嘉饌炸酥餅

材料： 外皮—麵粉６安
　　　　　　豬油一湯匙
　　　　　　沸水半杯

　　　　內皮—麵粉４安
　　　　　　豬油2½安
　　　　　　芝蔴洒面

　　　　餡—上肉４安　　　蝦肉４安
　　　　　　馬蹄６隻　　　甘笋一安
　　　　　　冬菇２隻　　　芫茜２棵
　　　　　　葱粒一湯匙

調味： 鹽半茶匙　　　糖半茶匙
　　　　生抽２茶匙　　古月粉少許
　　　　蔴油少許　　　豆粉一茶匙

製法： ① 麵粉６安篩在大盆中，冲入沸
　　　　　水迅速搞匀，加入豬油搓成一
　　　　　軟團。
　　　　② 另粉４安篩在桌上，放入豬油
　　　　　搓成另一軟團。
　　　　③ 蝦肉用鹽水洗淨以布吸乾水份
　　　　　，切成小粒。

④ 上肉洗淨剁成肉醬、甘笋、馬
　蹄皆以羗磨磨幼。
⑤ 冬菇洗淨蒸熟切幼、芫茜及葱
　洗淨切粒。
⑥ 將所有餡料放入深桶內，加調
　味料拌匀撻至起膠。
⑦ 取出兩份粉團、搓成長條，各
　切十六塊小團、將外皮按扁包
　入內皮，輾成長條向外捲起，
　將長卷分由左右邊向內摺叠、
　再以木棍輾成中厚外薄之圓形
　、將一份餡料放入後,四週打褶
　收口，按扁成圓餅、塗上清水
　或蛋液，滾滿芝蔴。
⑧ 燒熱半鑊油，文火將餅放入炸
　至金黃色。

Chopsticks Crisp

INGREDIENTS:

OUTER PASTRY—

6 oz. flour
½ cup boiling water
1 tbsp. lard

INNER PASTRY—

4 oz. flour
2½ oz. lard
Sesame seeds for coating

FILLING—

4 oz. pork
4 oz. shelled shrimp
6 water chestnuts
1 oz. carrot
2 dried mushrooms
2 sprigs of parsley
1 tbsp. chopped green onion

SEASONINGS:

½ tsp. salt
½ tsp. sugar
2 tsp. light soy
dash of pepper
dash of sesame oil
1 tsp. corn starch.

METHOD:

1. Sift 6 oz. flour into mixing bowl, stir in boiling water vigorously. Add in lard and knead into a soft dough.
2. Sift another 4 oz. flour on table, add in lard to knead into a second soft dough.
3. Wash shelled shrimps in salted water. Dry and chop for further use.
4. Wash and chop pork. Grate carrot and water chestnut.
5. Wash, steam and dice mushrooms, wash and chop parsley and green onion.
6. Put all ingredients for filling into deep bowl, add in seasonings, mix well and pound until firm.
7. Knead both soft dough into 2 long rolls, cut each roll into 16 equal portions. Flatten outer pastry to wrap in inner one. Roll into a rectangular strip. Half turn and repeat once. Knead into a round. Wrap in filling, draw edge to seal, then flatten with rolling pin. Brush on water and roll the whole cake with sesame seeds.
8. Bring half a pan of oil to the boil and deep fry crisps over medium heat until golden brown.

棗蓉金露酥

材料：　皮—麵粉10安　　　發粉2茶匙
　　　　　　　豬油4安　　　　糖4安
　　　　　　　蛋2隻

　　　　　餡—棗蓉1小罐
　　　　　　　另蛋液1隻塗面
　　　　　　　欖仁20粒裝飾

製法：　①麵粉、發粉一同篩在桌上，中
　　　　　　間開窩。
　　　　　②豬油，糖及打勻之蛋同放在穴
　　　　　　中拌溶。逐少將四週麵粉撥入
　　　　　　以手反覆按之。
　　　　　③將按勻之軟粉團切成二十等份
　　　　　　，用手搓圓，捏成小窩，將棗
　　　　　　蓉放在窩中後收口。收口處向
　　　　　　下貼上墊紙一張，排放焗盤中。
　　　　　④每個酥面塗上蛋液，頂上放欖
　　　　　　仁一粒點綴。
　　　　　⑤焗爐預先開定二百度，將全盤
　　　　　　餅放入中格焗約廿五分鐘至金
　　　　　　黃色即可取出。

Date Jam Crisp

INGREDIENTS:

PASTRY—

10 oz. flour
2 tsp. baking powder
4 oz. lard
4 oz. sugar
2 eggs

FILLING—

1 small can date jam
1 beaten egg
20 olive kernels

METHOD:

1. Sift flour and baking powder on the table, make a well in the centre.
2. Put in lard, sugar and beaten eggs and mix well. Slowly stir in flour a little at a time, and knead into a smooth dough.
3. Roll the dough into a long roll and cut into 20 even portions. Knead each portion into a round ball and flatten. Wrap date jam filling in each pastry case. Draw edges together.
4. Brush beaten egg on the surface. Put an olive kernel on top of each cake, and a piece of square paper at the bottom.
5. Bake in pre-set oven of 200° F for 25 minutes until golden brown.

REMARKS: Any kind of sweet paste can be used for filling.

椰茸炸酥盒

材料： 外皮—麵粉10安
水5安
油2½安

內皮—麵粉6安
豬油3½安

餡—椰茸半杯
花生⅓杯
芝蔴2湯匙
糖1杯

製法： ① 麵粉十安篩在桌上開穴、中放豬油及水搓溶，慢慢撥入四週之麵粉搓成軟團，以濕布蓋住。

② 另麵粉6安篩在桌上，加入豬油搓勻成團。

③ 花生炒香去衣以木棍輾碎，芝蔴洗淨炒香與花生碎、椰茸及糖和勻放碗中候用。

④ 桌上洒粉少許作焙，將外皮及內皮兩份軟團各搓成長條分切成三十二等份，再將一份外皮包裹住一份內皮，用木棍向外輾成長形捲起。將長卷向外再輾一次捲起，重複兩次然後將捲起麵團打橫切為二份，切開處即有圓圈花紋露出，將花紋向下置桌上稍輾薄，放入椰茸餡，把另一半麵團同樣輾薄蓋上，花紋在上。然後揑緊四週鎖邊。

⑤ 鑊中放油燒熱，將火轉慢、酥盒放入油中炸至浮起，色澤微黃即可撈出。

Flaky Coconut Patty

INGREDIENTS:

OUTER PASTRY—

10 oz. flour
5 oz. water
2½ oz. oil

INNER PASTRY—

6 oz. flour
3½ oz. lard

FILLING—

½ cup dessicated coconut
1/3 cup peanuts
2 tbsp. sesame seeds
1 cup sugar

METHOD:

1. Sift 10 oz. flour on table and make a well in the middle. Place lard and water in well. Fold in flour and knead into a soft dough as outer pastry. Leave aside and cover with cloth.
2. Sift another 6 oz. flour on the table and knead with lard into a second soft dough as inner pastry.
3. Fry peanuts and remove skin. Crush into fine grains. Wash and saute sesame seeds. Put sesame seeds, peanuts, dessicated coconut and sugar together in a bowl.
4. Sift a little flour on table. Roll outer and inner pastries into 2 long rolls, divide both into 32 equal portions. Press an outer pastry to wrap in an inner one. Seal and roll into a long strip and roll it up. Give pastry a half turn and repeat twice. Cut the rolled pastry into 2 portions. Place a patterned side facing downwards and roll pastry into flat circle. Put in a spoonful filling and cover up with another flat circle with pattern facing upwards. Press the edges together and seal firmly.
5. Pour oil in a pan, slowly bring to boil. Then lower the heat and put in patties to deep fry until light brown.

五彩皮蛋酥

材料： 外皮—麵粉６安
水２安
豬油1½安
內皮—麵粉４安
豬油2½安
餡—蓮蓉10安
皮蛋２隻
蘇羌２安

製法： ①將外皮用之麵粉篩在桌上開窩
，放入水及豬油搓溶、慢慢撥
入四週麵粉，輕輕按勻搓成軟
團候用。
②另將麵粉４安篩在桌上與豬油
和勻。
③將外皮與內皮皆搓成長條切成
十六等份。把外皮按扁包入內
皮，揑緊邊沿以木棍輾長捲起
。打橫再輾長捲起，共捲２次
。將皮按薄成橢圓形。
④每隻皮蛋切爲８份，旁邊放蘇
羌一片以蓮蓉包裹之。放在餅

皮上揑起收口，將收口處向
墊紙一張，塗上蛋液放焗盤
⑤焗爐開定二百度，將皮蛋酥
入中格慢火焗半小時。

Thousand Years Egg Crisp

INGREDIENTS:

OUTER PASTRY—

6 oz. flour
2 oz. water
1½ oz. lard

INNER PASTRY—

4 oz. flour
2½ oz. lard

FILLING—

2 thousand years eggs
2 oz. preserved ginger
10 oz. lotus seed paste.

METHOD:

1. Sift 6 oz. flour on the table. Make a well in the middle. Add water and lard then mix well. Slowly stir in flour and knead into a smooth dough. Roll and cut into 24 equal pieces.
2. Knead 4 oz. flour with lard into another soft dough.
3. Roll and cut both doughs into 16 equal portions. Slightly press the outer pastry and put a piece of inner pastry on the top. Wrap up and press with a rolling pin. Roll into a long thin piece. Roll up like a jelly roll. Give pastry a half turn then roll up again. Repeat once. Press into an oval.
4. Cut each thousand years egg into 8 parts. Wrap it up with a little lotus seed paste and ginger. Fill each flattened pastry with filling. Draw edges together to enclose. Face sealed edge downward.
5. Brush beaten egg yolk on cake. Put in preheated oven of 200° F for ½ an hour.

REMARKS: Thousand Years Egg can be substituted by preserved egg yolk, or can be omitted.

鬆脆合桃酥

材料： 麵粉10安　　梳打粉½茶匙
　　　　臭粉½茶匙　　豬油4安
　　　　糖6安　　　　蛋1隻
　　　　合桃適量

製法： ①麵粉與梳打粉一同篩在桌上，中間開穴放入臭粉、豬油、糖、及蛋。

②先用豬油及蛋搓溶沙糖及臭粉、然後慢慢撥入麵粉以手反覆按勻。搓成長條，用刀分切卅二至四十等份，大小隨意。

③合桃去壳，把肉挑出，放入沸水中稍滾。倒起隔去水份，撕去衣膜吹乾，切成合桃粒待用。

④將小塊粉團用手搓圓後再按扁，以手指在餅中央按一小孔。餅面塗上一層打勻之蛋黃，合桃粒放在小孔中，排放在洒上麵粉之焗盤上。

⑤焗爐開定二百五十度，將整盤餅放入中格、焗十分鐘後，餅

已發大瀉開、即將焗爐開至百度再焗約十分鐘至餅面呈黃色即可取出。

Walnut Crisp

INGREDIENTS:

10 oz. flour
¼ tsp. soda
¼ tsp. ammonia powder
4 oz. lard
6 oz. sugar
1 egg (beaten)
several walnuts
another egg yolk for brushing

METHOD:

1. Sift flour and soda on the table. Make a hollow in the centre and put in ammonia powder, lard, sugar and beaten egg and mix together.
2. Work in dry ingredients and knead into a long roll then cut into 32 to 40 even portions.
3. Shell and boil walnuts. Drain and remove skin. Break into pieces for further use.
4. Roll each portion of the soft dough into a ball and flatten a little between palms. Press a small hole in the middle of the pastry with the thumb. Brush a layer of beaten egg yolk on top and put a piece of walnut in the hole. Sprinkle flour on baking tin and place crisps on tin.
5. Put tin in preheated oven of 250° F for 10 minutes. Increase heat to 300° F for another 10 minutes and bake until golden brown.

叉燒焗酥餅

材料： 皮—麵粉10安　　　牛油3安
　　　　　　豬油2½安　　　沙糖2安
　　　　　　水1安　　　　　蛋王1隻塗面

　　　　餡—叉燒6安　　　　洋葱3安
　　　　　　冬菇2隻　　　　甘笋1安
　　　　　　薑王1安

調味： 鹽⅓茶匙　　　　糖½茶匙
　　　　蠔油½茶匙　　　酒½茶匙
　　　　古月粉少許

製法： ①麵粉篩在桌上、開窩、放入牛
　　　　油、豬油、沙糖。先將油糖混
　　　　合、慢慢將四週麵粉撥入。邊
　　　　撥邊加水逐漸搓成一軟團、放
　　　　入雪柜候用。
　　　　②叉燒切指甲片、洋葱切幼粒、
　　　　冬菇浸透蒸熟切幼粒、薑王切
　　　　粒、甘笋出水後切指甲片。
　　　　③燒紅鑊加油慢火爆香洋葱至微
　　　　黃、加入叉燒、冬菇、甘笋各
　　　　粒兜炒後、贊酒以調味品和勻

、用生粉半茶匙開水及蠔油拌
　獻撈勻。最後加薑王拌妥放雪
　柜半小時。
④將粉團從雪柜取出、搓成長條
　、切為廿四或卅二等份、大小
　隨意、餡料亦由雪柜取出。
⑤將每份粉團開成圓形、中厚外
　薄。餡料一份放在中央、捏妥
　收口、將收口處向下以手按成
　小圓餅。塗上打勻之蛋王、排
　放焗盤上。
⑥焗爐開定二百度、將整盤酥餅
　放入中格焗約二十分鐘、至金
　黃色即可取出。

Cha Shiu Crisp

INGREDIENTS:

PASTRY—

10 oz. flour
3 oz. butter
2½ oz. lard
2 oz. sugar
1 oz. water
1 beaten egg yolk for brushing

FILLING—

6 oz. cha shiu
3 oz. onion
2 mushrooms
1 oz. carrot
½ oz. white leek

SEASONINGS:

½ tsp. salt
½ tsp. sugar
½ tsp. oyster sauce
½ tsp. wine
dash of pepper

METHOD:

1. Sift flour on table and make a hollow in centre, put in butter, lard and sugar. Mix oil with sugar. Slowly work in flour, adding water at the same time and knead into a soft dough. Put into refrigerator for further use.
2. Dice cha shiu and onion. Soak, steam and dice mushrooms. Dice carrot after boiled. Chop white leeks.
3. Heat a pan with oil, saute onion until light brown. Add in cha shiu, mushrooms and carrot to fry. Sprinkle wine and seasonings, mix well. Dissolve ½ tsp. cornstarch in water, add in oyster sauce to form gravy. Finally mix with chopped white leek and put into refrigerator.
4. Knead soft dough into long roll. Cut into 24 or 32 equal portions.
5. Knead each portion into a thin round, wrap in filling with sealed edge facing down. Flatten with palm and brush beaten egg yolk on top. Place onto baking sheet.
6. Put cake into preheated oven of 200° F for 20 minutes until golden brown.

千層老婆餅

材料： 外皮—筋粉５安　　麵粉５安
　　　　　　　糖２安　　　　豬油４安
　　　　　　　水５安

　　　　內皮—麵粉４安　　汀麵１茶匙
　　　　　　　豬油２安

　　　　餡—糖冬瓜１磅　　芝蔴¼杯
　　　　　　沙糖½杯　　　水½杯
　　　　　　羔粉¾杯　　　油數滴

製法： ①芝蔴用白鑊文火慢慢炒香，盛起。
　　　　②糖冬瓜放入肉搞中搞成醬，邊搞邊加入芝蔴。
　　　　③將糖加入瓜蓉內，慢慢流入水份搞勻。然後篩入羔粉拌好，最後加油數滴和勻候用。
　　　　④筋粉、麵粉同篩在桌上開穴。
　　　　⑤豬油、糖同放在中央，加水把糖拌溶再將麵粉撥入搓勻擦透。放置一旁。
　　　　⑤另麵粉４安加汀麵篩在桌上，加入豬油按勻擦滑。
　　　　⑥將內、外皮皆搓成長條分切卅二小團，每粒外皮包入一粒內皮，以木棍輾薄成一長條形，向外捲出。打橫分三節叠起。
　　　　⑦將每份粉團以手捏成窩，放入餡料包住，收口處向下貼紙一張。用手壓扁再以棍輾平使成餅形，以叉刺孔或用刀在中央割一刀。蛋王掃面，用二百度火焗至金黃色，約廿至卅分鐘。

Winter Melon Crisp

INGREDIENTS:

OUTER PASTRY–

5 oz. high protein flour ● 5 oz. plain flour ● 2 oz. sugar

4 oz. lard ● 5 oz. water

INNTER PASTRY–

4 oz. flour ● 1 tsp. wheat starch ● 2 oz. lard

FILLING–

1 lb. candied winter melon ● ¼ cup sesame seeds ● 1/3 cup sugar

½ cup water ● ¾ cup cooked glutinous rice flour ● few drops of oil

METHOD:

1. Fry sesame seeds over low heat and dish.
2. Mince candied winter melon and sesame seeds in mincer.
3. Put sugar into minced candied winter melon. Stir in water gradually and sift in cooked glutinous rice flour. Add in few drops of oil and mix well.
4. Sift plain flour and high protein flour together on table and make a hollow in centre. Put lard and sugar in centre, stir in water gradually to dissolve sugar. Slowly work in flour and knead into a soft dough as outer pastry.
5. Sift another 4 oz. flour with wheat starch on table, add in lard to knead into a second smooth dough.
6. Knead both doughs into 2 long rolls and cut each into 32 equal portions. Wrap in one portion of inner pastry with outer pastry, and roll into a long thin strip. Roll up strip, flatten a bit, then overlap both sides towards centre.
7. Knead pastry into a round, put in filling and pinch edges together. With sealed end facing down, stick a piece of paper at the bottom. Press with palm and roll until flatten. Use a fork to punch holes on top of the cake, brush on beaten eggs. Bake in oven of 200° F for 20-30 minutes, until golden brown.

蝦米沙葛餅

材料： 粉漿—麵粉2杯　　水1½杯
　　　　　生粉半杯　　　鷄蛋1隻
　　　　　發粉2茶匙　　豬油½杯
　　　　　鹽1茶匙

　　　　餡料—沙葛8安　　鹽½茶匙
　　　　　蝦米2安　　　古月粉半茶匙
　　　　　葱一條　　　　五香粉一茶匙

製法： ①麵粉、生粉、發粉一同篩在大碗中。加入鹽、鷄蛋及水和勻，最後加入豬油液拌成濃粉漿。

②沙葛去皮洗淨，刨成幼絲，用鹽稍醃後揸去水份，。

③蝦米洗淨切碎，剁幼成茸。

④葱洗淨切碎、將沙葛絲、蝦米茸及調味品加入一同拌勻。

⑤油一鍋燒沸，將長柄油提放入浸熱，取出倒去油加入粉漿小半勺，放沙葛絲在中央，然後再加麵粉漿蓋在沙葛絲之上，放入油鍋中炸片刻，粉漿發後即自動退出油提外，繼續至金黃色即可撈出。

Carrot Cake

INGREDIENTS:

BATTER—

2 cups flour
½ cup cornstarch
2 tsp. baking powder
1 tsp. salt
1½ cup water
1 egg
½ cup melted lard

FILLING—

8 oz. carrot
2 oz. dried shrimp
1 green onion
½ tsp. salt
1 tsp. mixed spice
½ tsp. pepper

METHOD:

1. Sift flour, cornstarch and baking powder together into mixing bowl. Mix well with salt, water and beaten egg. Add in lard and blend into a thick batter.
2. Peel, wash and grate carrot.
3. Wash, soak and chop dried shrimp.
4. Wash and chop green onion. Add in carrot, chopped shrimp, seasonings and mix well.
5. Pour oil in deep frying pan and bring to the boil. Put in long handled cake mould to heat for a while. Drain oil and half fill mould with batter. Add in carrot mixture then cover it up with another layer of batter. Dip mould in oil to deep fry until cake comes out from mould. Continue frying until golden brown. Drain.

REMARKS: Shredded cabbage may be substituted for carrot.

香脆葱油餅

材料： 麵粉10安　　　　　味精¼茶匙
　　　　鹽½茶匙　　　　　油2湯匙
　　　　糖¼茶匙　　　　　水½杯

　　　　餡—生豬油3安
　　　　　　葱2安
　　　　　　芝蔴半杯

製法： ①麵粉篩在桌上，中開一穴放入
　　　　　鹽、糖、味精和勻。加油及水
　　　　　拌溶後撥入麵粉搓成軟團。
　　　　②生豬油以暖水洗淨切幼丁、葱
　　　　　洗淨亦切幼粒、芝蔴洗淨吹乾
　　　　　候用。
　　　　③將軟麵團分成大小隨意之等份
　　　　　，四份至十份皆可，輾開成方
　　　　　形薄片、把部份豬油丁及葱粒
　　　　　平均舖在麵片上，再向外捲成
　　　　　長條圓筒，以手搓至稍幼。
　　　　④將幼長條捲成蛇餅狀、（即蚊
　　　　　香形），以木棍稍爲輾平，餅
　　　　　面塗水少許，滾上白芝蔴。

⑤平鍋燒熱加油少許，將圓餅
　入慢火烘5分鐘，反轉再烘
　分鐘，至兩邊金黃即可。

Green Onion Coil

INGREDIENTS:

10 oz. flour
½ tsp. salt
¼ tsp. sugar
¼ tsp. MSG
2 tbsp. oil
½ cup water

FILLING—

3 oz. pork fat
2oz. green onion
½ cup sesame seeds

METHOD:

1. Sift flour on the table, make a hollow in centre. Put in salt, sugar and MSG to mix well. Add in water and oil, stir together and slowly work in flour to knead into a smooth dough.
2. Wash pork fat in warm water and dice. Wash and chop green onions. Wash and dry sesame seeds for further use.
3. Divide soft dough into 4 to 10 equal portions. Roll each portion into a thin square, sprinkle diced pork fat and green onions evenly on top. Knead into a long thin roll.
4. Coil up the thin strip into a round. Use rolling pin to flatten. Brush on a little water and sprinkle evenly with sesame seeds.
5. Heat an oiled pan, put in one coiled round at a time to fry for 5 minutes. Turn over to fry the other side until both sides become golden brown.

家鄉煎薄餅

材料： 粉漿—麵粉10安　　糖１茶匙
　　　　　蝦醬２茶匙　　　鹽½茶匙
　　　　　水2½杯　　　　　豬油３湯匙
　　　　　梳打粉½茶匙

配料： 叉燒５安　　　　　蔴油½茶匙
　　　　　蝦仁５安　　　　　古月粉少許
　　　　　笋１安　　　　　　韮菜３安

製法： ①麵粉、梳打粉同篩在盆中。
　　　　　②蝦醬加水調勻，加入鹽、糖拌
　　　　　　好倒入粉料中，加豬油搞勻。
　　　　　③叉燒切指甲片、蝦仁切粒、韮
　　　　　　菜洗淨切粒、笋出水後切指甲
　　　　　　片、一同加入粉糊中、洒入古
　　　　　　月粉蔴油拌勻候用。
　　　　　④平鑊燒紅，掃油少許在上，倒
　　　　　　入粉糊一壳、文火煎香後，反
　　　　　　轉再煎至兩面黃，鏟起置碟中
　　　　　　，同樣煎其餘粉糊至全部煎完
　　　　　　為止。

備註： 蝦仁可以２安蝦米代之

Chinese Savoury Pancake

INGREDIENTS:

BATTER—

10 oz. flour
½ tsp. soda
2 tsp. shrimp paste
2½ cups water
½ tsp. salt
1 tsp. sugar
3 tbsp. lard

FILLING—

5 oz. cha shiu
5 oz. shrimp
3 oz. leek
1 oz. carrot
dash of pepper
½ tsp. sesame oil

METHOD:

1. Sieve plain flour and soda into mixing bowl.
2. Put shrimp paste in water, mix well and add seasonings. Stir until well blended. Pour into dry ingredients, add oil and stir again.
3. Chop cha shiu in thin pieces, wash and mash leeks. Boil and dice carrot. Wash and chop shrimps. Put together into batter, add in pepper and sesame oil then mix well.
4. Heat a pan and brush a little oil. Pour ¼ cup batter onto pan. Set pancake for a while, toss and brown the otherside.

REMARKS: 2oz.dried shrimp can substitute for fresh shrimp.
Leek can be replaced by parsley.

香甜水晶餅

材料： 皮─汀麵７安
　　　　　糯粉３安
　　　　　糖４湯匙
　　　　　清水１杯
　　　　　豬油４湯匙

　　　　餡─蓮蓉５安
　　　　　咸蛋王２隻

製法： ①汀麵與糯米粉混合篩勻在大盆中。
　　　　②水與糖同放鍋內用中火煮溶，糖溶後將沸糖水沖入混合粉料中以木棍搞勻，加入豬油同搓至軟。
　　　　③咸蛋王蒸熟切成十二粒、蓮蓉分成十二份搓圓。
　　　　④將軟粉團搓成長條，切成十二等份，以手壓扁放入蛋王一粒，再放蓮蓉一份，收口將餅壓扁。
　　　　⑤餅模內塗油，將粉團放入壓實、用力將餅敲出。
　　　　⑥蒸籠內塗油，將餅排放在內，猛火蒸八至十分鐘，離火後即呈透明狀。

44

Crystal Cake

INGREDIENTS:

PASTRY—

7 oz. wheat starch
3 oz. glutinous rice flour
4 tbsp. sugar
1 cup water
4 tbsp. lard

FILLING—

5 oz. lotus seed paste
2 preserved egg yolks

METHOD:

1. Sift wheat starch and glutinous rice flour in a mixing bowl.
2. Boil water with sugar. Pour boiling liquid into sifted flour. Stir with wooden spoon. Add lard and knead until soft.
3. Steam preserved egg yolks. Divide both egg yolks and sweet paste into 12 portions.
4. Roll the dough into long roll then cut into 12 equal portions. Press with palm and fill each round flattened pastry with egg yolk and sweet paste. Draw edges and seal well.
5. Put stuffed cake in greased wooden mould. Turn mould upside down and strike hard on table several times until the cake falls out.
6. Arrange cakes into greased steamer. Steam over high heat for 8 minutes. Cakes become transparent when cooled.

REMARKS: Lotus seed paste can be substituted by any kind of sweet paste.

荔芋肉茸餅

材料： 荔甫芋10安　汀麵１安　　中火炸至金黃色。
　　　　沸水1½安　五花肉８安
　　　　蝦米２安　冬菇３隻
　　　　芫茜葱各２棵

調味： 鹽１茶匙　　　糖１茶匙
　　　　生抽２茶匙　雞精½粒
　　　　古月粉½茶匙　麻油½茶匙
　　　　乾麵粉１杯

製法： ①荔芋去皮洗淨放蒸籠內蒸熟，
　　　　　取出最軟部份十安。
　　　　②汀麵沖入沸水搞匀搓成軟團。
　　　　③五花肉洗淨切成大片。
　　　　④冬菇蝦米洗淨浸透剁爛。芫茜
　　　　　、葱洗淨切粒。
　　　　⑤將荔芋、汀麵團及豬肉片同放
　　　　　肉搞中搞爛。加入冬菇蝦米粒
　　　　　及芫茜、葱粒稍搓。將調味品
　　　　　放入搞匀。
　　　　⑥將混合物取出做成圓餅形，滾
　　　　　上一層麵粉、放入熱油鍋中用

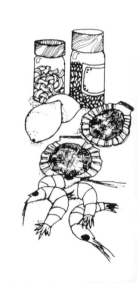

Taro Croquette

INGREDIENTS:

10 oz. taro
1 oz. wheat starch
1½ oz. boiling water
8 oz. pork
2 oz. dried shrimp
3 mushrooms
2 sprigs parsley
2 green onions

SEASONINGS:

1 tsp. salt
1 tsp. sugar
2 tsp. soy
½ chicken cube
½ tsp. pepper
½ tsp. sesame oil
1 cup flour for coating

METHOD:

1. Peel and wash taro, steam until soft. Use 10 oz. of the softest part.
2. Pour boiling water into wheat starch then stir and mix into a soft dough.
3. Wash pork and cut into pieces.
4. Wash and soak dried shrimps and mushrooms for 30 minutes. Chop finely. Chop parsleys and green onions as well.
5. Put taro, wheat starch dough and pork into mincer and mince together. Take out and put into a mixing bowl. Add chopped ingredients then season to taste.
6. Turn mixture into small rounds, coated with flour. Put into boiling oil and deep fry over medium heat until golden.

脆皮鮮蝦盒

材料：

| 皮—汀麵10安 | 沸水10安 |
| 鹽½茶匙 | |

脆漿—麵粉1杯	發粉1茶匙
生粉2湯匙	油1安
水½杯	鹽¼茶匙

| 餡—瘦肉6安 | 蝦肉6安 |
| 冬笋肉2安 | 葱一條 |

調味：

鹽½茶匙	糖½茶匙
生抽1茶匙	生粉1茶匙
古月粉少許	麻油½茶匙

製法：

①汀麵放在大盆中，沸水加鹽和勻沖入粉內搞勻，以蓋蓋住五分鐘後搓成軟團。

②瘦肉、蝦肉、冬笋肉皆切成幼粒，加調味品試味後再加切碎葱粒和勻。

③將粉團分作4等份再搓成長條，切為小粒，以刀或木棍開成薄圓形。

④將圓粉皮放在左手中，放入餡一份，以另一塊圓皮蓋上。捏緊邊沿做成圓盒狀，排放塗油蒸籠內。

⑤鑊中煮滾半鑊水，將蒸籠放在上面大火蒸5分鐘。

⑥麵粉、生粉、鹽同篩在盆中，加水和勻後再加油拌搞片刻，將蒸熟蝦盒加入沾上脆漿，放入熱油鍋中炸至金黃色。

Crispy Meat Pie

INGREDIENTS:

PASTRY—

10 oz. wheat starch
10 oz. boiling water
½ tsp. salt

FILLING—

6 oz. lean pork
6 oz. shrimp
2 oz. bamboo shoot
1 green onion

SEASONINGS:

½ tsp. salt
½ tsp. sugar
1 tsp. light soy
1 tsp. corn flour
dash of pepper
½ tsp. sesame oil

COATING BATTER—

1 cup flour
1 tsp. baking powder
2 tbsp. corn flour
1 oz. oil
½ cup water
¼ tsp. salt

METHOD:

1. Boil water with salt and pour onto wheat starch in the mixing bowl and stir vigorously.
2. Dice shrimps, lean pork and bamboo shoot finely, add in seasonings and chopped green onions.
3. Divide wheat starch dough into 4 equal portions, then roll into long strips and cut into small pieces. Roll again into small rounds.
4. Put fillings onto each round, cover it up with another piece, seal edge firmly to enclose filling. Put in greased steamer.
5. Place steamer onto a pan of boiling water to steam for 5 minutes.
6. Sift flour starch and salt into a bowl, add water, oil and stir until well blended. Coat every pie with batter then put in boiling oil to deep fry until golden brown. Serve hot.

豬油炒米餅

材料： 炒米粉１０安　　　水１¼杯
　　　　沙糖１０安　　　　芫茜一棵
　　　　豬油６湯匙

製法： ①炒米粉篩在大盆內。
　　　　②預備深鍋一個，將水倒入與沙
　　　　　糖一同用文火煮沸。沸後加豬
　　　　　油煮溶。
　　　　③將沸糖水冲入炒米粉內，以木
　　　　　棍迅速搞勻。
　　　　④芫茜洗淨剁碎，加入粉料中，
　　　　　取出置桌上以手搓勻成軟團。
　　　　⑤餅模內塗油，將軟團放入按實
　　　　　，輕輕用模柄頂出。約可做廿
　　　　　四隻小餅。

Rice Flour Cookie

INGREDIENTS:

10 oz. fried rice flour
1¼ cups water
10 oz. sugar
6 tbsp. lard
1 sprig parsley.

METHOD:

1. Sift fried rice flour into mixing bowl.
2. Pour water in saucepan and bring to the boil after sugar is added. Stir in lard.
3. Add boiled solution into flour in mixing bowl and stir well.
4. Wash and chop parsley, then add to the mixture and knead into a soft dough. Divide into 24 pieces.
5. Grease cake mould, stuff a piece of dough into it. Press cake out.

生煎菜肉包

材料： 皮—麵種１０安　　豬油２湯匙
　　　　　水半杯　　　　鹼水 $\frac{1}{4}$ 茶匙
　　　　　麵粉１０安
　　　　　葱粒或黑芝蔴點綴

　　　　餡—瘦肉８安　　肥肉２安
　　　　　白菜８安

調味： 鹽一茶匙　　　糖 $\frac{3}{4}$ 茶匙
　　　　生抽一茶匙　　生粉一茶匙
　　　　古月粉少許　　蔴油少許

製法： ①麵種放在大盆中，加入豬油、
　　　　水及鹼水搓成流質將麵粉篩入
　　　　，搓成軟粉團，以布蓋住候用
　　　　。

　　　　②白菜洗淨，放入沸水中拖至半
　　　　熟，再放毛巾內扭乾切幼。

　　　　③豬肉洗淨切幼再稍剁碎，與白
　　　　菜拌勻後加入調味品搞拌撈妥
　　　　。

　　　　④桌上洒以少許麵粉，將軟粉團
　　　　取出搓成長條，對切成四十八

等份。

⑤將每件皮料搓圓按扁成中厚
薄之圓形，放入肉餡捏成包
。包面掃上清水，洒以葱粒
黑芝蔴。

⑥平底鍋放在爐上燒熱，加油
許，將包子排放在內，文火
之。不時洒以清水，蓋上鍋
焗約七分鐘即成。

Vegetable Meat Pie

INGREDIENTS:

PASTRY—

10 oz. pre-made yeast dough
2 tbsp. lard
½ cup water
¼ tsp. alkali water
10 oz. flour

FILLING—

8 oz. lean pork
2 oz. fat pork
8 oz. Chinese cabbage
Chopped green onion or black sesame for garnishing.

SEASONINGS:

1 tsp. salt
¾ tsp. sugar
1 tsp. light soy
1 tsp. corn starch
dash of pepper
dash of sesame oil

METHOD:

1. Put yeast dough in a large mixing bowl, add in lard, water and alkali water, stir into a fluid. Sift in flour, knead into a soft dough. Leave aside and cover with cloth.
2. Wash Chinese cabbage, put in boiling water for a short while. Dry with clean towel and cut into fine pieces.
3. Wash and dice pork, chop into smaller pieces. Mix chopped pork with cabbage and add in seasonings.
4. Sprinkle a little sifted flour on table, roll soft dough into long roll and cut into 48 even portions.
5. Flatten each small dough into a round. Put in filling. Draw edges to seal. Brush the top with water and sprinkle chopped green onions or black sesame seeds.
6. Heat frying pan till hot and add oil, place buns in and fry with medium heat. Add a little water from time to time. Finally put on lid and leave for 7 minutes. Serve hot.

酥皮蓮蓉包

材料：　皮—麵種８安　　　沙糖３安
　　　　　　豬油一湯匙　　　臭粉半茶匙
　　　　　　鹼水½茶匙　　　水２湯匙
　　　　　　麵粉４安　　　　發粉１茶匙

　　　　酥心—麵粉２安　　　豬油一安

　　　　餡—蓮蓉半磅

備註：

麵種—發子一茶匙溶於半杯溫水中，放置十分鐘後倒入半磅篩之麵粉窩中，搓成軟團。用布住置溫暖地方發十二至十五小方可取用。

製法：　①將麵種放在大盆中，加沙糖、豬油、臭粉、鹼水及清水搓溶成流質。麵粉、發粉放在篩內篩入混合物中搓成軟麵團，將麵團搓成長條分切二十等份。
　　　　　②另麵粉二安篩在桌上與豬油搓成軟團。搓成長條亦分切二十等份。
　　　　　③將每份外皮按薄包入一粒酥心，壓緊邊沿用木棍輾成長條，然後捲起。如是重覆兩次。最後將粉團稍輾薄成圓形，將蓮蓉包入、收口向下，貼上白紙一張。置蒸籠內猛火蒸八分鐘。

54

Sweet Paste Bun

INGREDIENTS:

OUTER PASTRY—

8 oz. yeast dough
3 oz. sugar
1 tbsp. lard
½ tsp. ammonia soda
¼ tsp. alkali water
2 tbsp. water
4 oz. flour
1 tsp. baking powder

INNER PASTRY—

2 oz. flour
1 oz. lard

FILLING—

8 oz. lotus seed paste

METHOD:

1. Put yeast dough in a mixing bowl, add in sugar, lard, ammonia soda, alkali water and water to mix into fluid form. Sift flour and baking powder onto fluid and knead into soft dough. Knead into long roll and cut into 20 equal portions.
2. Sift another 2 oz. flour on table and knead into soft dough with lard. Cut into 20 equal portions as inner pastry.
3. Wrap one portion of inner pastry inside one portion of outer pastry, seal securely. Knead into long thin strip and roll up. Give pastry a half turn, repeat once, then roll into a small round. Wrap in lotus seed paste, with sealed edge facing downward. Stick a piece of paper at the bottom with water. Put in steamer to steam over high heat for 8 minutes.

REMARKS: Yeast dough should be made 12-15 hours before.
First, dissolve a tsp. dried yeast into ½ cup warm water. Pour solution into ½ lb. sieved flour and knead into a soft dough. Cover up and put in a warm place for 12-15 hours.

蠔油叉燒飽

材料： 包皮—麵粉４安　　　發粉一茶匙
　　　　　麵種８安　　　　沙糖３安
　　　　　臭粉半茶匙　　　鹼水細半茶匙
　　　　　豬油一湯匙　　　水一至二湯匙

　　　　餡料—叉燒８安　　　蠔油一湯匙
　　　　　糖一茶匙　　　　生抽一茶匙
　　　　　葱粒一湯匙　　　生粉２湯匙
　　　　　清水４湯匙

製法： ①麵種放在大盆中，加沙糖、臭
　　　　粉、鹼水、豬油及水一齊搓匀
　　　　。

　　　②麵粉、發粉同篩在桌上開穴，
　　　　將已搓開之麵種混合料倒入穴
　　　　中，撥入麵粉搓成軟麵團，放
　　　　置一旁。

　　　③叉燒切指甲片。

　　　④燒紅鑊，加油少許煮沸，倒入
　　　　上湯大半杯加調味和匀，慢慢
　　　　將生粉水加入煮成濃獻。加入
　　　　叉燒及葱粒撈匀盛起攤凍，可
　　　　放雪柜中雪一小時。

⑤麵團取出搓成長條，以刀切
　廿四等份，按薄後將叉燒餡
　在包皮中央，右手執起包皮
　密摺收口，飽底墊以白紙。

⑥蒸籠放在沸水鍋上，將包子
　入猛火蒸約八分鐘。

Cha Shiu Bun

INGREDIENTS:

PASTRY—

8 oz. yeast dough
3 oz. sugar
½ tsp. ammonia powder
¼ tsp. alkali water
1 tbsp. oil
2 tbsp. water
4 oz. flour
1 tsp. baking powder

FILLING—

8 oz. cha shiu (roast pork)
1 tbsp. oyster sauce
1 tsp. sugar
1 tsp. light soy
2 tbsp. corn flour
4 tbsp. water
1 tbsp. chopped green onion

METHOD:

1. Put yeast dough, baking powder, sugar, ammonia powder and alkali water into a big bowl. Add water gradually and rub the dough into liquid form.
2. Sift flour and baking powder on a clean table, make a hole in the middle. Add in yeast dough mixture. Knead in flour to turn into a soft dough.
3. Dice cha shiu for further use.
4. Heat a pan, add oil and pour in ¾ cup of stock. Put in seasonings. Mix 3 tbsp. water with cornstarch in pan and stir until thickened. Add in cha shiu and diced green onion to mix well. Remove from pan and put in the refrigerator for a while.
5. Roll soft dough into long strip and cut into 24 even portions. Flatten each portion into a flat circle. Put filling in the middle and wrap it up. Stick a piece of small square paper at the bottom of each bun.
6. Place steamer over boiling water in a pot and steam the buns with strong fire for 8 minutes.

肉餡小籠飽

材料： 麵粉10安　　　　　　沸水½杯
　　　　凍水１安

　　　　餡—枚肉８安　　　　　肥肉２安
　　　　冬菇２隻　　　　　　　蔥２條
　　　　芫茜１棵

調味： 鹽½茶匙　　　　　　　糖１茶匙
　　　　生抽１茶匙　　　　　　酒１茶匙
　　　　蔴油少許　　　　　　　古月粉少許
　　　　生粉１茶匙加水２湯匙

製法： ①麵粉篩入大盆中，把沸水迅速
　　　　　冲入用木棍搞勻。
　　　　②桌上洒麵粉少許作粉焙，將麵
　　　　　團倒出，用凍水將手弄濕搓麵
　　　　　團至軟滑。
　　　　③枚肉肥肉洗淨一同剁爛、冬菇
　　　　　浸透切幼，芫茜及蔥皆洗淨切
　　　　　幼，一齊放在深盆內加調味品
　　　　　和勻撻至起膠，生粉水邊撻邊
　　　　　加。
　　　　④將麵團搓成長條，分切爲廿四

至卅二等份，以木棍輾成薄圓
形。
⑤將圓薄包皮放平在手中，加入
餡料一份，打摺捏成包形。
⑥蒸籠內舖以洗淨菜葉，將包子
排放在上，置沸滾鑊上猛火蒸
十五分鐘。

Steamed Meat Bun

INGREDIENTS:

10 oz. flour
1 cup boiling water
1 oz. cold water

FILLING—

8 oz. lean pork
2 oz. fat pork
2 mushrooms
1 green onion
1 sprig parsely

SEASONINGS:

½ tsp. salt
1 tsp. sugar
1 tsp. light soy
1 tsp. wine
dash of sesame oil
dash of pepper
1 tsp. cornstarch + 2 tsp. water

METHOD:

1. Sift flour into mixing bowl, stir in boiling water. Mix thoroughly.
2. Sift a little extra flour on table. Pour mixture out. Wet hand with cold water then knead mixture into a soft dough.
3. Wash and mince pork. Soak and dice mushrooms. Wash and chop green onion and parsley. Put ingredients into deep bowl, add in seasonings and pound until firm. Adding in cornstarch solution while pounding.
4. Knead soft dough to a long roll. Divide into 24 or 32 equal portions. Roll into thin rounds.
5. Place round on left hand. Put filling in centre, pinch edges together to form a bun.
6. Place a few pieces of vegetable leaves in steamer. Arrange buns on top and steam for 5 minutes. Serve hot.

什錦糯米卷

材料： 皮—麵粉10安　　　發粉2茶匙
　　　　臭粉¼茶匙　　　糖3安
　　　　豬油1½茶匙　　　溫水½杯
　　　　餡—糯米飯一杯　　臘腸2條
　　　　臘肉2安　　　　冬菇2隻
　　　　蝦米一安　　　　芫茜少許

調味： 鹽½茶匙　　　　　糖1茶匙
　　　　生抽半茶匙　　　豬油1湯匙

製法： ①麵粉發粉同篩在桌上，中間開
　　　　穴。將臭粉、糖、豬油放入穴
　　　　中。逐少把溫水加入拌溶，慢
　　　　慢撥入麵粉搓勻成軟團。以半
　　　　濕毛巾蓋住發廿分鐘。
　　　　②臘腸、腊肉、冬菇皆洗淨蒸熟
　　　　切粒。
　　　　③蝦米浸透剁爛成茸。
　　　　④燒紅鑊，倒入生油一湯匙爆香
　　　　葱頭棄去，將蝦米放入爆炒片
　　　　刻　加腊味冬菇一同炒勻盛起
　　　　候用。

⑤糯米飯加入豬油及腊味粒撈
　，調妥味。
⑥洒粉焙於桌上，然後將麵團
　在桌上以木棍輾成長方形，
　4吋×6吋，厚½吋，把糯
　飯放在長方近身的一邊，向
　捲出。收口處向下，以紙墊
　。
⑦鑊中水煮至大滾後，將糯米
　放於蒸籠內轉放鑊上蒸8分
　，取出切件熱食。

Glutinous Rice Roll

INGREDIENTS:

PASTRY—

10 oz. flour
2 tsp. baking powder
¼ tsp. ammonia powder
3 oz. sugar
1½ tsp. lard
½ cup warm water

FILLING—

1 cup cooked glutinous rice
2 Chinese preserved sausages
2 oz. preserved meat
2 dried mushrooms
1 oz. dried shrimps
a sprig of Chinese parsley

SEASONINGS:

½ tsp. salt
1 tsp. sugar
½ tsp. light soy
1 tbsp. lard

METHOD:

1. Sift plain flour and baking powder on the table, make a hole in the middle. Put ammonia powder, sugar and lard in the hole. Adding warm water in gradually, knead to a soft dough. Use a towel to cover the dough, leave to rise for 20 minutes.
2. Wash and steam preserved sausages, preserved pork, and mushrooms. Soak dried shrimps in water until soft.
3. Dice all steamed materials, chop dried shrimps finely.
4. Heat a pan until hot, add 1 tbsp. oil. Add in shallot and fry, discard. Put all ingredients in the pan and saute. Leave aside for further use.
5. Add lard and other ingredients to cooked rice. Put in seasonings and mix well.
6. Dust the table with a little flour, put dough on and roll to an oblong 4" x 6". Place filling on one side. Roll out to seal. Put a piece of paper underneath.
7. Place all the rolls in steamer, put onto a pan of boiling water to steam for 8 minutes. Take out and cut into pieces. Serve hot.

省時腊腸卷

材料： 皮——麵粉10安　　發粉2茶匙
　　　　臭粉½茶匙　　豬油一湯匙
　　　　糖4安　　　　溫水4安

　　　　餡——臘腸數對

製法： ①麵粉與發粉同篩在桌上，中間開穴，放入臭粉、豬油、糖，用一半溫水將穴內各物拌溶。其餘溫水慢慢加入，邊加邊將四週麵粉撥入，直至和成軟麵團。以半乾濕布蓋着待發廿分鐘。

②臘腸洗淨，切成二吋長度候用。

③將粉團取出，用木棍開成長方形、厚約1½分，用刮刀分切成2吋×3½吋之長方小塊。

④將臘腸橫放在長方小塊的一邊。然後向外捲起，收口處向下，墊紙一張。

⑤猛火煮滾半鑊水，將一格蒸籠放入。臘腸卷排放另一格蒸中放在上面，猛火蒸十二至五分鐘。

Chinese Sausage Roll

INGREDIENTS:

10 oz. flour
2 tsp. baking powder
¼ tsp. ammonia powder
1 tbsp. lard
4 oz. sugar
4 oz. warm water

FILLING—

Several pairs of Chinese sausage

METHOD:

1. Sift flour and baking powder on clean table, make a hollow in the centre, put in ammonia powder, lard and sugar. Use half of the warm water to stir the ingredients in the hollow until dissolved. Add in the second half gradually, meanwhile work in the flour and knead into a smooth dough. Cover with damp cloth and leave aside for 20 minutes.
2. Wash preserved sausages, and cut into 2 inch portions for further use.
3. Roll the soft dough into 1/8 inch thick, cut into 2" x 3½" rectangles.
4. Put sausage on one side of the pastry and roll towards centre. Put a small piece of paper at the bottom with the sealed edge facing down.
5. Boil half pan of water and put in a steamer. Place sausage rolls in another steamer and put on top of the first one. Steam over high heat for 12-15 minutes.

REMARKS: If other cooked sausages are used, cooking time will be shortened to 8 minutes.

蛋煎班戟卷

材料： 皮—麵粉2杯　　古月粉少許
　　　　　　鹽半茶匙　　鷄蛋5隻
　　　　　　水3杯

　　　　餡—叉燒5安　　銀芽8安
　　　　　　靑瓜3安　　甘笋3安
　　　　　　冬菇2隻

調味： 鹽半茶匙　　　　糖半茶匙
　　　　生抽一茶匙　　生粉半茶匙
　　　　古月粉少許

製法： ①麵粉、鹽、古月粉同篩於大盆
　　　　　　中。
　　　　②鷄蛋去壳加水打勻，慢慢倒入
　　　　　　粉中打滑。
　　　　③燒紅煎鍋，以油掃塗油燒熱。
　　　　　　倒入粉漿½杯攤平，慢火煎至
　　　　　　粉漿凝結時，反轉煎至微黃即
　　　　　　可取出，以碟盛起，全部約有
　　　　　　十六至十八張。
　　　　④叉燒切絲，靑瓜切絲，甘笋飛
　　　　　　水後切絲，冬菇浸透蒸熟亦切

絲。
⑤燒紅鑊，加油煮沸，倒入銀
　爆炒片刻兜起。
⑥再燒紅鑊，加油爆炒靑瓜、
　笋絲、隨即加入叉燒、冬菇
　銀芽兜炒片刻，調妥味後以
　粉水打獻炒勻盛起攤凍。
⑦班戟平放桌上，將餡料放在
　邊，向外捲出，兩邊摺入繼
　至成長條形，以蛋液貼住收
　處。
⑧另打蛋液3隻，將班戟卷放
　塗勻。轉放燒沸之淺油鍋內
　至兩面金黃色。

Savoury Pancake Roll

INGREDIENTS:

PASTRY—

2 cups flour
½ tsp. salt
5 eggs
3 cups water
dash of pepper

FILLING—

5 oz. cha shiu (roast pork)
8 oz. bean sprouts
3 oz. cucumber
3 oz. carrot
2 dried mushrooms

SEASONINGS:

½ tsp. salt
½ tsp. sugar
1 tsp. light soy
½ tsp. corn flour
dash of pepper

METHOD:

1. Sift flour, pepper and salt into a mixing bowl.
2. Mix beaten eggs with water in a separate bowl then pour into the flour. Whisk until smooth.
3. Heat a little oil in frying pan and pour in about ¼ cup of batter to cover bottom of pan. Cook until brown on under side, then loosen edges to turn and brown the other side. Turn on to a plate.
4. Boil and shred carrot. Soak mushrooms until soft, steam and shred. Also shred cha shiu and cucumber.
5. Heat pan and add in oil, saute bean sprouts, remove from pan and leave aside.
6. Heat pan again, put in oil and saute cucumber, mushrooms, cha shiu and bean sprouts together. Add in seasonings and use corn starch solution to make gravy. Remove from pan and let cool.
7. Place pancake flat on table, put in filling on one side and roll towards centre. Fold in both sides, continue to roll until it forms a narrow envelope. Brush on egg to seal.
8. Beat 3 eggs in bowl and dip pancake roll in. Put in frying pan and fry with a little oil until both sides are golden brown.

REMARKS: Cha Shiu can be substituted by luncheon meat or ham while bean sprouts can be replaced by shredded cabbage.

三絲炸春卷

材料： 春卷皮半磅　　叉燒３安
　　　　雞絲３安　　　肉絲３安
　　　　冬菇３隻　　　甘筍２安
　　　　銀芽８安

調味： 鹽１茶匙　　糖１茶匙
　　　　生抽１茶匙　酒１茶匙
　　　　古月粉少許　麻油½茶匙
　　　　生粉２茶匙

製法： ①叉燒切絲，冬菇浸透蒸熟切絲
　　　　　、甘筍去皮焓熟切絲。
　　　　②雞絲、肉絲用三份一調味品醃
　　　　　十分鐘後，泡油隔乾候用。
　　　　③燒紅鑊加油煮沸，倒入銀芽爆
　　　　　炒片刻，盛起候用，再燒紅鑊
　　　　　加入三種肉絲爆香，加冬菇、
　　　　　甘筍絲，倒入銀芽再加調味品
　　　　　兜勻，以生粉開水打濃獻拌勻
　　　　　攤凍。
　　　　④春卷皮攤開，將餡料二湯匙左
　　　　　右放在一邊，向外捲起，收口
　　　　　處以豆粉水塗之。
　　　　⑤鑊燒紅，注入油半鍋煮至大
　　　　　時即將春卷放入，中火炸至
　　　　　黃色。

Spring Roll

INGREDIENTS:

½ lb. spring roll pastry
3 oz. cha shiu or ham
3 oz. chicken (shredded)
3 oz. pork (shredded)
3 dried mushrooms
2 oz. carrot or bamboo shoot
8 oz. bean sprouts

SEASONINGS:

1 tsp. salt
1 tsp. sugar
1 tsp. light soy
1 tsp. wine
dash of pepper
¼ tsp. sesame oil
2 tsp. corn starch.

METHOD:

1. Soak and steam mushrooms. Peel, boil and shred carrot. Shred cha shiu and mushrooms.
2. Season shredded chicken and pork with 1/3 seasonings for 10 minutes. Leave aside.
3. Boil oil in a hot pan, saute bean sprouts for further use.
4. Heat pan with oil again and pour in shredded meat to saute. Add in mushrooms, carrot, bean sprouts and seasonings. Mix well with corn starch and water solution and let cool.
5. Put pastry flat on the table, add in 2 tbsp. of filling and roll towards centre. Use corn starch solution to seal.
6. Pour oil in a heated pan, put spring rolls in boiling oil to deep fry until golden brown.

REMARKS: Bean sprout can be substituted by shredded cabbage.
Dried mushroom can be replaced by fresh one.

三絲蒸粉卷

材料： 皮—沙河粉10安（約為3張）
每張剪開4段
炒香芝蔴2湯匙

餡—雞肉3安　　　豬肉3安
叉燒4安　　　銀芽5安
冬菇2隻　　　甘筍2安

調味： 鹽一茶匙　　　糖一茶匙
生抽一茶匙　　古月粉少許
上湯半杯　　　生粉一茶匙

製法： ①雞肉切絲用羗汁、酒及生粉各
少許撈勻醃片刻，泡油候用。
②豬肉切絲用部份生抽、鹽、糖
、酒、生粉、油撈勻醃片刻，
泡油候用，叉燒切絲。

③冬菇洗淨泡軟蒸熟切絲，甘筍
出水後切絲。
④燒紅鑊，加油，放入葱頭爆香
棄去，倒入銀芽爆炒。加入甘
筍冬菇炒片刻，倒下其他肉絲
兜勻。加調味品續炒。以上湯
開生粉打獻拌勻盛起攤凍。
⑤沙河粉舖在桌上，將一份餡料
放在一旁，包住向外捲起。收
口向下，排放碟上。
⑥將碟子放入蒸籠，猛火蒸5分
鐘。取出洒上芝蔴及生抽、熟
油、熱食。

Rice Flour Sheet Roll

INGREDIENTS:

PASTRY–

10 oz. rice flour sheet (about 3 pieces, each cut into 4 portions)
2 tbsp. fried sesame seeds

FILLING–

3 oz. chicken meat ● 3 oz. pork ● 4 oz. cha shiu ● 5 oz. bean sprout
2 dried mushrooms ● 2 oz. carrot

SEASONINGS :

1 tsp. salt ● 1 tsp. sugar ● 1 tsp. light soy ● dash of pepper
½ cup stock ● 1 tsp. cornstarch

METHOD:

1. Shred chicken and marinade with a little ginger juice, wine and cornstarch for a while. Deep fry in warm oil.
2. Shred pork and marinade with a little light soy, salt, sugar, wine, cornstarch, and oil. Deep fry in warm oil for further use.
3. Shred cha shiu. Wash, steam and shred mushrooms. Boil and shred carrot.
4. Heat a pan with oil, saute shallot and discard. Pour in bean sprouts and saute. Add in carrot, mushrooms, chicken and pork to saute. Put in seasonings, use corn starch and stock solution to make gravy. Dish out and let cool.
5. Place rice flour sheet flat on table, put a portion of filling on one side, wrap in and roll towards centre. Put sealed edge facing fown, then arrange on plate.
6. Put plate into steamer and steam for 5 minutes. Take out and sprinkle on sesame seeds, light soy and oil. Serve hot.

牛油焗布甸

材料： 水2½杯　　糖10安
　　　　牛油４安　　麵粉３安
　　　　粟粉３安　　吉士粉２安
　　　　花奶２杯　　鷄蛋４隻

製法： ①將兩杯半清水放入鍋中，加入
　　　　糖及牛油一同煮溶。
　　　②麵粉、粟粉及吉士粉一同篩在
　　　　大盆中，花奶加入將粉拌勻。
　　　③鷄蛋去壳打爛留用。
　　　④煮溶之糖水大滾後，將火收慢
　　　　。加入粟粉漿慢慢搞勻，加完
　　　　後再滾即可離火。
　　　⑤離火加蛋搞勻，轉倒在玻璃兜
　　　　或不銹鋼兜內。
　　　⑥焗爐預早開定四百五十度，將
　　　　布甸坐在一盆水中放入焗爐約
　　　　十五分鐘至面焦黃即可取出。

Butter Pudding

INGREDIENTS:

2½ cups water
10 oz. sugar
4 oz. butter
3 oz. plain flour
3 oz. corn starch
2 oz. custard powder
2 cups milk
4 eggs

METHOD:

1. Boil 2½ cups of water together with sugar and butter until dissolved.
2. Sift flour, corn starch and custard powder in a big bowl. Add in milk and blend into a smooth batter.
3. Beat eggs for further use.
4. Reboil sugar solution, add in batter stirring continously until thickened. Remove from fire.
5. Add in well beaten eggs and whisk until smooth. Pour into a greased baking tin.
6. Set oven to 450° F. Put baking tin in a basin half filled with water. Bake until golden brown.

焗西米布甸

材料： 西米10安　　　水４杯
　　　　糖２杯　　　　牛油４安
　　　　花奶１杯　　　粟粉４安
　　　　吉士粉１安　　椰汁２杯
　　　　鷄蛋４隻

製法： ①西米用清水浸數小時。
　　　　②鍋中放水半鍋，煮沸後將西米
　　　　　倒入煮至透明，轉放凍水中泡
　　　　　凍洗去膠質，隔去水份。
　　　　③上列水４杯置鍋中，加糖煮溶
　　　　　後，放入牛油及花奶搞勻，隨
　　　　　即將西米倒入拌勻。
　　　　④粟粉，吉士粉與椰汁混和，慢
　　　　　慢加入沸糖水中。邊加邊搞，
　　　　　至完全加完後，再滾即可離火
　　　　　。
　　　　⑤離火後加入已打勻之蛋搞透，
　　　　　倒在玻璃兜內放入焗爐中，以
　　　　　四百五十度火焗至淺棕色。

Sago Pudding

INGREDIENTS:

10 oz. sago
4 cups water
2 cups sugar
4 oz. butter
1 cup milk
4 oz. corn starch
1 oz. custard powder
2 cups coconut juice
4 eggs

METHOD:

1. Soak sago well in water for few hours.
2. Pour sago into a pan of boiling water and simmer until transparent. Wash under running tap. Drain and leave aside.
3. Put 4 cups of water in a saucepan. Add sugar, slowly bring to the boil. When sugar has dissolved, blend in butter and milk. Pour in sago, stirring until well blended.
4. Mix coconut juice with corn starch and custard powder. Gradually stir into boiling sugar mixture. Continue stirring until thickened. Remove from fire.
5. Add in well beaten eggs. Whisk until smooth. Pour into a fire-proof container and put in the middle shelf of preheated oven with 450° F. Bake until golden brown.

REMARKS: Coconut juice can be subsituted by half water and half milk.

蛋黃豆沙粽

材料：糯米２０安　　　　鹼水２湯匙
硼砂½茶匙　　　　油２湯匙
粽葉６安　　　　　水草一束
餡—豆沙１０安　　咸蛋王３隻

製法：①糯米洗淨浸透、隔清水份。加
入鹼水、硼砂及油一同撈勻候
用。
②咸蛋王每隻分做４份，用豆沙
包裹着候用。
③粽葉水草置沸水中煮片刻，取
出洗淨抹乾。
④將三塊粽葉舖在左手中，薄薄
舖上一層糯米。把包裹蛋王之
豆沙稍爲壓扁放在米上，再舖
糯米一層，將兩邊粽葉摺起覆
入，用水草鬆動地紮住　搖動
粽子，以能聽見米粒移動之聲
响爲原則。
⑤深鍋內墊粽葉數片，將包好之
粽子排放在內，注入凍水蓋過
粽面，猛火煮沸後轉用中火續

恰６小時，趁熱撈起攤凍，食
時加糖膠。

Red Bean Paste Dumpling

INGREDIENTS:

20 oz. glutinous rice
2 tbsp. alkali water
¼ tsp. borax
2 tbsp. oil

FILLING—

10 oz. red bean paste
3 preserved egg yolk
6 oz. bamboo leaves
a bunch of straw

METHOD:

1. Wash and soak glutinous rice with water. Drain. Mix well with alkali water, borax and oil.
2. Cut each preserved egg yolk into quarters, wrap each quarter with red bean paste.
3. Boil bamboo leaves and straw for few minutes. Wash thoroughly then dry with towel.
4. Put 3 sheets of leaves on left hand, add in a thin layer of rice. Slightly press bean paste and lay on rice. Cover paste with another thin layer of rice. Draw leaves together and tie up loosely.
5. Put few pieces of bamboo leaves at bottom of deep saucepan, arrange dumplings on top. Cover up with cold water. Put over high heat and bring to boil. Continue boiling over medium heat for 6 hours. Take dumplings out while still hot. Serve together with syrup.

加料裹蒸粽

材料：糯米２１安　　　開邊綠豆１磅
　　　咸蛋黄１０隻　　　燒鴨１０件
　　　冬菇１０隻　　　　五花肉２０件

調味：鹽３茶匙　　　　糖２茶匙
　　　五香粉２茶匙　　　古月粉½茶匙
　　　鷄精½粒　　　　　油３湯匙
　　　蓮葉１０張　　　　粽葉３０片
　　　水草２０條

製法：①五花肉切件加鹽及五香粉醃兩
　　　　　天。
　　　②糯米洗淨，隔去水份。加入鹽
　　　　　二茶匙、糖一茶匙、鷄精及油
　　　　　撈勻。
　　　③綠豆用水浸透、淘去豆殼，加
　　　　　鹽一茶匙、糖一茶匙撈勻。
　　　④冬菇浸透去蒂留用。
　　　⑤蓮葉粽葉以沸水浸透洗淨，隔
　　　　　去水份並用毛巾抹乾，先將一
　　　　　張蓮葉舖在桌上，再加粽葉三
　　　　　片，隨即放糯米一層，跟着放

綠豆一層，然後放入咸蛋王兩
隻、五花肉、燒鴨、冬菇各二
件，分別排好，蓋上一層綠豆
之後再蓋一層糯米，將粽葉、
蓮葉覆入包成四方形，用水草
紮妥。
⑥深鍋放粽葉數片墊底，將粽放
入，加水蓋過粽面。猛火保沸
後轉用中火焗七小時，趁熱捞
起攤凍。

Luxurious Rice Dumpling

INGREDIENTS:

21 oz. glutinous rice
1 lb. green beans
10 preserved egg yolks
10 pieces of roasted duck
10 mushrooms
20 pieces pork belly
10 pieces of lotus leaves
20 pieces of straw
30 pieces of bamboo leaves

SEASONINGS:

3 tsp. salt
2 tsp. sugar
2 tsp. mixed spice
½ tsp. pepper
½ chicken cube
3 tbsp. oil

METHOD:

1. Strip pork belly and marinade with spice powder and salt for two days.
2. Wash glutinous rice and drain. Mix well with 2 tsp. salt, 1 tsp. sugar, 1 chicken cube; oil and pepper.
3. Soak green beans in water, remove skin, add in 1 tsp. salt and 1 tsp. sugar.
4. Soak mushrooms and remove stalk.
5. Wash lotus leaves and bamboo leaves and soak in boiling water till soft. Drain and dry with towel. Place 3 pieces of bamboo leaf on a piece of lotus leaf. Put a layer of glutinous rice first and place green beans as second layer. Then put 2 preserved egg yolks, together with 2 pieces of pork belly, 2 pieces of roasted duck and 2 mushrooms on top. Then cover with a layer of green beans and another layer of glutinous rice. Fold in leaves to form a square and tie firmly with straw.
6. Prepare a deep pot and place several pieces of bamboo leaves at the bottom. Put in rice dumplings. Fill water in to cover up all the dumplings. Use high heat to bring water to boil and then reduce fire and continue boiling for another 7 hours. Take out and drain.

脆皮油炸粽

材料：糯米１磅　　　開邊綠豆半磅
　　　　五花肉８安　　硼砂半茶匙

調味：鹽２茶匙　　　糖２茶匙
　　　　生油３湯匙　　酒一湯匙
　　　　五香粉一湯匙　古月粉半茶匙

脆漿：麵粉２杯　　　生粉２湯匙
　　　　發粉３茶匙　　水一杯
　　　　豬油半杯　　　鹽少許

製法：①糯米洗淨浸透，隔清水後加入
　　　　　鹽１茶匙，生油２湯匙，糖１
　　　　　茶匙及硼砂用手撈勻。
　　　　②綠豆用溫水浸數小時後以箵箕
　　　　　淘去豆殼，隔清水份，加鹽半
　　　　　茶匙、糖半茶匙，生油一湯匙
　　　　　撈勻。
　　　　③五花肉切骨牌形，燒紅鑊放入
　　　　　豬肉，用餘下之鹽糖加五香粉
　　　　　、古月粉贊酒爆香。
　　　　④粽葉用沸水泡軟洗淨，每二塊

摺成一個三角兜，放米兩湯匙
，再放綠豆一湯匙，加入豬肉
後蓋上另一湯匙綠豆及二湯匙
米，將粽葉摺入包攏，以水草
紮緊。
⑤深鍋內放水大半鍋，鍋底放粽
葉數片，將包好之粽子排放在
上。猛火焓約六小時，撈起打
開。
⑥麵粉、生粉、發粉篩入盆中，
加清水、豬油、鹽搞勻。將打
開粽子對角介成四角，放入粉
漿中沾上粉料。
⑦鍋中倒入油半鍋，煮至大熱時
將粽放入炸至金黃色。

Rice Dumpling Fritter

INGREDIENTS:

1 lb. glutinous rice
½ lb. green beans
8 oz. pork belly
½ tsp. borax

SEASONINGS:

2 tsp. salt
2 tsp. sugar
3 tbsp. oil
1 tbsp. wine
1 tbsp. mixed spice
½ tbsp. pepper

BATTER:

2 cups flour
2 tbsp. corn starch
3 tsp. baking powder
1 cup water
½ cup lard
a little salt

Bamboo leaves and straw for wrapping.

METHOD:

1. Wash and soak glutinous rice in water. Drain and mix with 1 tsp. salt, 2 tbsp. oil, 1 tsp. sugar and borax.
2. Soak green beans in warm water for few hours and remove shell. Mix with ½ tsp. salt, ½ tsp. sugar and 1 tbsp. oil after drained.
3. Cut pork belly, put in hot pan, and saute with remaining salt, sugar, spicy powder, pepper and wine.
4. Wash bamboo leaves and soak in boiling water till soft. Drain and place two leaves together and fold into a triangle shape. Put 2 tbsp. rice, 1 tbsp. green beans and fill centre with pork. Cover up with another tbsp. green beans and 2 tbsp. rice again. Fold in leaves and tie firmly with straw.
5. Cook about 6 hours in boiling water. Drain and put aside.
6. Sift flour, baking powder and corn flour into a mixing bowl. Add in water, lard, salt and stir well. Cut untied dumpling into 4 quarters.
7. Dip quartered rice dumplings into batter and deep fry in hot oil till golden brown.

REMARKS: Borax can be omitted if it is hard to get.

錦繡糯米雞

材料： 皮—糯米10安　　鹽1茶匙
　　　　　豬油1湯匙　　荷葉5塊

　　　　　餡—叉燒4安　　枚肉4安
　　　　　冬菇5隻　　　甘筍2安
　　　　　鷄肉5件

調味： 鹽半茶匙　　　糖1茶匙
　　　　　蠔油1茶匙　　生抽1茶匙
　　　　　酒1茶匙　　　古月粉少許

製法： ①糯米浸數小時後，以筲箕隔去
　　　　　水份，用大量沸水淋兩次。
　　　　②蒸籠內放薄布一方，將淋透糯
　　　　　米倒入排好蒸半小時，盛起加
　　　　　鹽及豬油把飯撈勻。
　　　　③枚肉切粗粒用部份調味撈過泡
　　　　　油候用。
　　　　④鷄件亦以部份調味品加羗汁半
　　　　　茶匙撈勻泡油候用。
　　　　⑤叉燒切粗粒、冬菇浸透蒸熟切

開、甘筍飛水切片。
⑥燒紅鑊加油少許，贊酒倒入上
湯半杯，將用剩調味料加生粉
半茶匙、水一茶匙和勻加在上
湯中煮成獻，將餡料加入獻中
拌勻盛起攤凍。
⑦荷葉用沸水浸透洗淨抹乾，攤
在桌上，先舖一層薄糯米飯，
放入部份餡料，中放鷄件及冬
菇，蓋上另一層糯米飯。將荷
葉摺入包好，置蒸籠內大火蒸
十五分鐘熱食。

Steamed Rice Dumpling with Assorted Meat

INGREDIENTS:

PASTRY—

10 oz. glutinous rice
1 tsp. salt
2 tbsp. lard
5 pieces of lotus leaves

FILLING—

4 oz. cha shiu
4 oz. lean pork
5 mushrooms
2 oz. carrot
5 pieces of chicken

SEASONINGS:

½ tsp. salt
1 tsp. sugar
1 tsp. oyster sauce
1 tsp. light soy
1 tsp. wine

METHOD:

1. Soak glutinous rice for few hours, drain and pour on boiling water. Repeat once.
2. Place a piece of cloth in steamer. Pour in glutinous rice and steam for ½ an hour. Remove from steamer, add in salt, lard and mix well.
3. Cut lean pork into pieces, add in part of the above seasonings and saute well.
4. Marinade chicken with a little seasonings and ½ tsp. ginger juice. Saute for further use.
5. Cut cha shiu into pieces. Soak, steam and cut each mushroom into halves. Boil and chop carrot.
6. Heat a pan with little oil. Pour in wine and ½ cup stock. Add in the left seasonings. Mix ½ tsp. cornstarch with 1 tsp. water to cook into gravy. Stir well with filling and let cool.
7. Soak lotus leaves in boiling water, wash and dry. Place flat on table, put on a layer of glutinous rice, add in part of the filling with chicken and mushrooms. Cover with another layer of rice on top. Fold lotus leaves to wrap into a dumping, put into steamer to steam over high heat for 15 minutes. Serve hot.

椰蓉糯米糍

材料： 皮—糯米粉8安
　　　　清水⅘杯
　　　　汀麵2安
　　　　沸水2安
　　　　豬油2安
　　　　糖1½安
　　　餡—椰茸4安
　　　　花生4安
　　　　糖8安
　　　　紅車里子數粒
　　　　糕粉作焙

製法： ①糯米粉篩在桌上開穴，逐少倒
　　　　入清水搓成軟團。
　　　②汀麵篩在盆中，將沸水冲入用
　　　　木棍迅速搞勻。
　　　③糯米粉團加入汀麵盆中一同搓
　　　　透，倒入豬油及糖再搓勻。
　　　④蒸籠塗油，切出混合粉團三份
　　　　之二放入猛火蒸15分鐘，取出
　　　　與其餘三份之一生粉團混合搓
　　　　勻。

⑤花生炒香去衣後輾碎，加入椰
　茸、糖一同拌勻。
⑥將混合粉團分成卅二至四十零
　份。以糕粉作焙，用手捏成窩
　放入餡料，收口捏成飽形。
⑦將小糯米糍放在蒸籠內蒸三分
　鐘。取出滾上椰茸、頂上放切
　細車厘子一粒作裝飾。

Coconut Snow Ball

INGREDIENTS:

PASTRY—

8 oz. glutinous rice flour
¾ cup water
2 oz. wheat starch
2 oz. boiling water
2 oz. lard
1½ oz. sugar

FILLING—

4 oz. dessicated coconut
4 oz. peanut
8 oz. sugar
a few red cherries for decoration

METHOD:

1. Sift glutinous rice flour on table. Pour in water slowly and knead into soft dough.
2. Sift wheat starch in a mixing bowl. Pour in boiling water and stir well immediately.
3. Knead both doughs together with sugar and lard. Mix well.
4. Steam 2/3 of dough for 15 minutes. Take out and knead together with the other 1/3 dough.
5. Saute and grind peanuts. Mix with sugar and dessicated coconut for filling.
6. Cut dough into 32 to 40 small pieces. Press and shape into small nests and fill each with filling . Draw edges together to enclose.
7. Put snow balls into steamer and steam for 3 minutes. Decorate each with a piece of cut cherry.

REMARKS: Any kind of sweet paste can be used for filling.

豆沙煎軟糍

材料： 皮一汀麵２安
　　　　沸水３安
　　　　糯米粉８安
　　　　糖２安
　　　　豬油２安
　　　　水½杯至⅔杯
　　　餡一豆沙８安
　　　　咸蛋王２隻

製法： ①汀麵篩在大盆中，倒下沸水後
　　　　　隨即用木棍搞勻。
　　　　②糯米粉篩於桌上，中間開穴，
　　　　　放入糖、豬油，水及汀麵團一
　　　　　同用力搓勻。
　　　　③將已搓妥之粉團，切一半放在
　　　　　猛火蒸籠內蒸約八分鐘。取出
　　　　　與其餘一半生粉團搓勻候用。
　　　　④咸蛋王蒸熟，每隻切成十六粒
　　　　　，用豆沙包裹成波子大小之圓
　　　　　形。
　　　　⑤軟粉團搓成長條，切為三十二
　　　　　等份，每份小團以木棍輾成薄

圓形，中放豆沙，收口後壓扁
⑥平底鑊燒紅，加油少許，將小
圓餅放入煎至兩面金黃即可。

Sweet Paste Cookies

INGREDIENTS:

PASTRY—

2 oz. wheat starch
3 oz. boiling water
8 oz. glutinous rice flour
2 oz. sugar
2 oz. lard
½ to ¾ cup water

FILLING—

8 oz. red bean paste
2 preserved egg yolks

METHOD:

1. Sift wheat starch in a mixing bowl, pour in 3 oz. of boiling water, stir immediately.
2. Sift glutinous rice flour on table, make a hole in the centre. Put in sugar, lard, water, wheat starch dough and knead into a smooth dough.
3. Divide the dough into 2 halves, steam one half for 8 minutes. Take out and knead with the second half till soft then leave aside.
4. Steam preserved egg yolks. Cut into 16 cubes, use red bean paste to wrap into the shape of a marble.
5. Roll the smooth dough into a long roll and cut into 32 equal portions. Press each portion into a thin round pastry case, wrap in one marble-shaped red bean paste. Then seal the edges together. Flatten with palm.
6. Heat a pan, add in a little oil. Put in cakes and fry until both sides are golden brown.

REMARKS: A mixture of dessicated coconut and sauted sesame with sugar can be used for filling.

香滑紅豆沙

材料： 紅豆一磅　　清水8杯
　　　　片糖二十安　油4杯

製法： ①紅豆洗淨置鍋中，加清水8杯
　　　　煮約一小時半，如用壓力煲則
　　　　半小時即可。
　　　　②盛起豆沙，放入搞肉機中搞一
　　　　次搞碎豆殼。
　　　　③煲燒熱，放入水半杯煮沸，將
　　　　片糖加入煮溶，糖完全溶後即
　　　　可加入豆沙。
　　　　④豆沙加入後即以煲鏟不停搞拌
　　　　，邊搞邊加油，一直炒到豆沙
　　　　有七成乾，盛起放在深碟上攤
　　　　凍，放在完全密封之膠盒中，
　　　　隨時取用，約可保存兩個月。

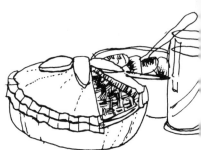

Red Bean Paste Filling

INGREDIENTS:

1 lb. red bean
8 cups water
20 oz. brown sugar slices
4 cups oil

METHOD:

1　Wash and place red beans in a deep saucepan, add in 8 cups water to simmer for 1½ hours. (Or use pressure cooker for ½ an hour).
2. Put cooked red beans in a meat mincer to turn into a smooth paste.
3. Heat a pan and boil ½ cup of water, put in brown sugar to boil until dissolved. Add in mashed red beans.
4. Stir red bean paste continously and add in oil. Continue stirring until red been paste is 70% dry. Remove from pan and let cool. Keep red bean paste in an air tight plastic container. Can be stored for more than 2 months in a Tupperware.

REMARKS: 2 oz. sugar can be added if you prefer a sweeter filling.

賀年蛋散仔

材料： 麵粉１０安　　　沙糖３安
　　　　豬油３安　　　　雞蛋２隻
　　　　清水一湯匙

製法： ①麵粉篩在桌上，中間開穴。
　　　　②將沙糖、豬油、雞蛋一同放在
　　　　　穴中拌勻。慢慢撥入四週麵粉
　　　　　，一邊加水、一邊搓成軟團。
　　　　③桌上洒乾粉少許，把麵團放在
　　　　　上面以木棍輾成長薄塊。將薄
　　　　　粉皮以刀介成半吋乘吋半之小
　　　　　長條，每塊長條中用剪刀剪一
　　　　　條縫，將一邊向縫反穿過去。
　　　　④將油半鍋煮至僅沸，把蛋散仔
　　　　　放入，文火炸至微黃色，以罩
　　　　　籬撈起，用紙吸去餘油。攤凍
　　　　　後以玻璃瓶盛起，隨時取食。

New Year Cruller

INGREDIENTS:

10 oz. flour
3 oz. sugar
3 oz. lard
2 eggs
1 tbsp. water

METHOD:

1. Sift flour on table, make a hollow in the centre.
2. Put sugar, lard, beaten eggs in hollow and work into a soft dough. Adding in water occasionally.
3. Sift a little flour on table, roll dough into a thin oblong. Using a knife or pastry wheel, cut strips ½" x 1½" long. Cut gash in centre of each, and twist end through.
4. Heat pan with oil. Put in crullers when oil is going to boil. Deep fry over low heat until golden. Take out and drain. Absorb oil with kitchen paper. Can be kept in air tight plastic box for more than one month.

脆炸馬蹄條

材料：馬蹄１磅　　　　　糖10安
　　　　水２杯　　　　　　花奶２杯
　　　　馬蹄粉６安　　　　豬油２湯匙

脆漿：麵粉１杯　　　　　發粉２茶匙
　　　　生粉１湯匙　　　　水半杯
　　　　豬油或生油３湯匙

製法：①馬蹄去皮洗淨磨碎，放鍋中加
　　　　　糖及水煮熟候用。
　　　　②花奶開馬蹄粉，隔去雜質，慢
　　　　　慢加入煮滾之糖水中，加入豬
　　　　　油，邊加邊搞。
　　　　③羔盆塗油，將混合物倒入，轉
　　　　　放猛火蒸籠內蒸四十分鐘，取
　　　　　出攤凍，放入雪柜過夜，取出
　　　　　切成長條。
　　　　④麵粉、發粉、生粉同篩於大盆
　　　　　中，慢慢注入水及油拌成粉漿
　　　　　，將馬蹄條放入沾滿粉糊。

⑤油一鑊燒至略沸時，即將火
　慢少許，把馬蹄條逐一放入
　至金黃色。

備註：馬蹄粉可用粟粉代替，
　　　　要加多一杯流質。

Water Chestnut Fritter

INGREDIENTS:

1 lb. water chestnut
10 oz. sugar
2 cups water
2 cups milk
6 oz. water chestnut powder
2 tbsp. lard

CRISP BATTER:

1 cup flour
1 tbsp. corn starch
2 tsp. baking powder
½ cup water
3 tbsp. lard

METHOD:

1. Peel and wash water chestnuts, grind and boil in water with sugar and lard.
2. Mix water chestnut powder with milk, then filter the solution.
3. Slowly stir the above mixture into boiling water.
4. Pour into oiled cake pan and steam for 40 minutes.
5. Pour ½ cup of water slowly into a mixture of sieved flour, cornstarch and baking powder. Stir in oil to make a smooth batter. Cut water chestnut pudding into fingers and dip in batter.
6. Bring oil to boil, then lower the heat. Add in coated pudding one by one. Deep fry until golden.

REMARKS: Cornstarch can be substituted for water chestnut powder with 1 cup liquid added.

酸甜炸雲吞

材料： 雲吞皮４安　　　蝦肉８安
　　　　瘦肉６安　　　　肥肉２安
　　　　冬笋２安　　　　雞蛋１隻

調味： 鹽一茶匙　　　　糖半茶匙
　　　　古月粉少許　　　豆粉一茶匙
　　　　麻油少許

獻料： 酸甜醋一杯
　　　　生粉一茶匙

製法：
①蝦肉洗淨後以毛巾吸乾水份，切成幼粒。
②瘦肉、肥肉洗淨亦切成幼粒。
③冬笋以沸水泡過後，切幼。
④將蝦肉、豬肉同放大碗中用手稍撻，隨後加入甘笋粒及蛋王、（蛋白留作收口用）加調味品攪勻。
⑤將餡料放在雲吞皮之一角，向內包入，用蛋白收口貼緊，置中火油鍋內炸至金黃色，用罩籬捞起放在碟上。
⑥酸甜醋煮沸，生粉開水少許入，搞拌成漿，以碗盛起，時蘸用、或將獻淋在炸雲吞亦可。

備註： 冬笋可用甘笋代替。

Sweet and Sour Won Ton

INGREDIENTS:

4 oz. won ton pastry

FILLING:

8 oz. shrimp (shelled)
6 oz. lean pork
2 oz. fat pork
2 oz. bamboo shoot
1 egg

SEASONINGS:

1 tsp. salt
½ tsp. sugar
dash of pepper
dash of sesame oil
1 tsp. corn flour

GRAVY:

1 cup sweet-sour sauce
1 tsp. corn starch

METHOD:

1. Shell shrimps and wash. Dry with towel, cut into cubes.
2. Cook bamboo shoots in boiling water. Drain and dice.
3. Wash lean pork and fat pork, drain and dice.
4. Put shrimp, lean pork and fat pork in mixing bowl, pound well. Add in bamboo shoot and beaten egg yolk. Put in seasonings and mix well.
5. Put filling at the corner of a piece of won ton pastry. Fold in pastry to enclose filling, seal with egg white. Deep fry in boiling oil till golden brown. Drain and place on dish.
6. Boil sweet-sour sauce. Mix corn starch with water and add in. Stir till thickened. Pour sauce on fried won ton and serve. (Or serve sweet sour sauce separately in a bowl.)

REMARKS: Carrot can be used in place of bamboo shoot.

芝蔴薯茸棗

材料： 番茨８安　　豬油１安
　　　　糯米粉６安　蓮蓉或豆沙８安
　　　　冰肉２安　　芝蔴½杯

製法： ①番茨去皮洗淨切件，放猛火蒸
　　　　　籠內蒸十五分鐘。
　　　　②取出夾爛成茸，加豬油同搓至
　　　　　軟，放在桌上。
　　　　③糯米粉用篩篩在茨茸上，搓成
　　　　　軟團，將軟團分成廿四等份。
　　　　④冰肉即用砂糖醃過兩三天之肥
　　　　　肉片取出切成幼粒，與蓮蓉混
　　　　　和成廿四條狀。
　　　　⑤將軟團置掌心壓扁成欖圓形，
　　　　　每件皮包入一件蓮蓉，捏好搓
　　　　　成長筒形。
　　　　⑥芝蔴洗淨隔乾水份，將茨茸棗
　　　　　放入滾上一層。
　　　　⑦燒紅鑊加油半鍋煮至將沸時，
　　　　　即將茨棗放入。改用文火炸至
　　　　　金黃色。

Sweet Potato Croquette

INGREDIENTS:

8 oz. sweet potato
1 oz. lard
6 oz. glutinous rice flour
8 oz. red bean paste
2 oz. candied pork
½ cup sesame seeds

METHOD:

1. Peel sweet potatoes, wash and cut into pieces. Put into steamer and steam for 15 minutes over strong fire.
2. Smash and add lard to knead until soft.
3. Put smashed sweet potato on the table and sift glutinous rice flour on it. Knead into a soft dough and cut into 24 equal portions.
4. Marinade fat pork slices with sugar for 2 or 3 days as candied pork. Mix red bean paste with diced pork. Knead into 24 short rolls.
5. Take one portion of the soft dough and flatten to oval shape between palms. Wrap in one roll of red bean paste, to make a cylindrical shape.
6. Wash and drain sesame seeds. Put in sweet potato roll to stick on one layer of seeds.
7. Heat a frying pan, half fill the pan with oil. When oil is hot, put in sweet potato rolls, reduce fire to deep fry until golden brown.

REMARKS: Potatoes can be used in place of sweet potatoes by adding 2 oz. sugar.

鷄絲銀針粉

材料： 銀針粉—汀麵４安　　沸水４½安
　　　　　　　　　鹽少許
　　　　配料—鷄腿１隻　　靑紅椒各１
　　　　　　　冬菇２隻　　銀芽６安
　　　　　　　葱蒜頭各１粒

調味： 鹽１茶匙　　　　　糖１茶匙
　　　　生抽２茶匙　　　　酒１茶匙
　　　　古月粉少許　　　　蔴油少許

製法： ①汀麵與鹽同篩在大盆中，將沸
　　　　　水冲入粉中以木棍搞勻，用蓋
　　　　　將盆蓋住五分鐘後，取出搓成
　　　　　軟粉團。
　　　　②將粉團搓成長條，切開成廿四
　　　　　等份，再將每份搓成筷子般長
　　　　　條，切開數段，將每段放在掌
　　　　　心搓至兩頭尖，放在塗油碟中
　　　　　猛火蒸五分鐘。
　　　　③鷄腿起肉切絲，用羗汁、酒各
　　　　　半茶匙及生粉一茶匙醃二十分
　　　　　鐘後泡嫩油候用。

④靑紅椒去籽切幼絲，冬菇浸
　蒸熟切幼絲候用，。
⑥燒紅鑊加油煮沸，放入葱頭
　蒜頭炸香，加靑紅椒爆炒片
　隨即倒入銀芽兜炒，跟着加
　鷄絲，銀針粉、熟冬菇各物
　同炒透，贊酒以調味品加入
　味，上碟。

Silver Pin Noodle with Shredded Chicken

INGREDIENTS:

Silver pin noodle—
    4 oz. wheat starch
    4½ boiling water
    dash of salt
1 chicken thigh
1 green pepper
1 red pepper
2 dried mushrooms
6 oz. bean sprouts
1 shallot
1 garlic

SEASONINGS:

1 tsp. salt
1 tsp. sugar
2 tsp. light soy
1 tsp. wine
dash of pepper
little sesame oil

METHOD:

1. Sift wheat starch and salt in a mixing bowl. Pour in boiling water and stir vigorously. Cover for 5 minutes then take out to knead into a smooth dough.
2. Roll the dough into a long roll, cut into 24 equal portions. Knead each portion into the shape of chopstick and cut into small cubes. Put each part between 2 palms and roll into pin-shaped noodles. Put silver pin noodles on a greased plate to steam for 5 minutes.
3. Remove bone and shred chicken thigh. Marinade meat for 20 minutes with ½ tsp. ginger juice, ½ tsp. chinese white wine and 1 tsp. corn starch. Deep fry with warm oil and leave aside.
4. Remove seeds from green and red peppers then shred. Soak mushrooms until soft, steam and shred for further use.
5. Heat a pan and add oil. Put in shallot and garlic, saute red and green peppers for a while then add in bean sprouts. Finally pour in shredded chicken meat, silver pin noodles and mushrooms. Saute altogether. Sprinkle with wine, add seasonings and serve hot.

百花芝蔴蝦

材料： 蝦肉１磅　　　　肥肉１安
　　　　芫茜２棵　　　　葱２條
　　　　麵包４片　　　　白芝蔴１杯

調味： 鹽一茶匙　　　　糖半茶匙
　　　　古月粉少許　　　蔴油數滴
　　　　生粉1½湯匙

製法： ①蝦挑去腸臟，用粗鹽洒在上面
　　　　置水喉下冲洗二三次，用乾毛
　　　　巾吸乾水份，攤開略吹乾。
　　　②肥肉焓熟過凍水，切成幼粒候
　　　　用。
　　　③芫茜及葱洗淨剁成幼粒。
　　　④方飽四片隔夜吹乾或放焗爐內
　　　　用慢火烘乾。
　　　⑤蝦肉用刀拍爛，放入深宛內
　　　　加調味和勻，用手撻至起膠，
　　　　邊撻邊加肥肉，芫茜葱及生粉
　　　⑥方飽片塗上生粉少許，將蝦膠
　　　　之四分一舖在上面，刮平後洒
　　　　滿芝蔴。

⑦燒紅鑊，倒入生油半鍋煮至
沸。將芝蔴蝦放入用文火炸
金黃色，撈起後一片切成四
至八個三角形，熱食。

Sesame Prawn Triangle

INGREDIENTS:

1 lb. prawn
1 oz. fat pork
2 sprigs parsley
2 green onions
4 pieces of bread
1 cup sesame seeds

SEASONINGS:

1 tsp. salt
½ tsp. sugar
dash of pepper
few drops of sesame oil
1½ tbsp. cornstarch

METHOD:

1. Devein prawns, wash with salt under running water. Dry with towel.
2. Boil fat pork for a while then wash with cold water. Chop into fine pieces.
3. Wash and chop parsley and green onion.
4. Put bread into very slow oven and bake until dried.
5. Mash prawns then put into mixing bowl with seasonings added. Pound against the bowl until elastic. Add in chopped pork, parsley and cornstarch. Mix well.
6. Put a little cornstarch onto bread, spread one quarter prawn mixture on top. Flatten with knife then coat with sesame seeds.
7. Pour oil in hot pan. When oil begins to boil, put in triangles and deep fry over medium heat until golden. Cut each square into 4 to 8 triangles. Serve hot.

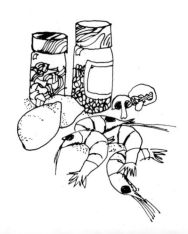

鮮肉餡湯丸

材料： 皮—糯米粉10安
水8至10安
鹽⅓茶匙

餡—枚肉½磅
馬蹄8隻
冬菇2隻
葱2條

調味： 鹽半茶匙　　糖半茶匙
豆粉半茶匙　　古月粉少許
水3湯匙　　　油1湯匙

製法： ①糯米粉篩在大盆中，加鹽及水
搓勻。
②枚肉洗淨切幼粒稍剁。馬蹄去
皮洗淨亦切幼粒，冬菇洗淨浸
透切幼，葱切粒。
③將調味品加入肉中撈勻撻透，
再把馬蹄、冬菇及葱加入搞勻。
④糯米粉團分成廿四至廿八等份
，以手弄成小窩，將一份餡料
放入，收口搓圓。

⑤鍋中放入上湯約三杯，加鹽
茶匙，油二湯匙煮沸，放入
丸煮至浮起，加入洗淨之生
片，再滾即可盛起。

Glutinous Rice Balls in Soup

INGREDIENTS:

PASTRY—

10 oz. glutinous rice flour
8-10 oz. water
¼ tsp. salt

FILLING—

½ lb. lean pork
8 water chestnuts
2 dried mushrooms
2 green onions

SEASONINGS:

½ tsp. salt
½ tsp. sugar
½ tsp. corn flour
3 tbsp. water
1 tbsp. oil
dash of pepper

METHOD:

1. Sift glutinous rice flour with salt in mixing bowl, add water and knead into soft dough.
2. Wash and dice lean pork. Peel and dice water chestnuts. Soak and dice mushrooms. Also chop green onions.
3. Put seasonings in meat and pound until firm. Add in water chestnuts, mushrooms, green onions and mix well.
4. Divide dough into 24 to 28 portions. Press each portion into the shape of a nest. Then put in filling and wrap up. Roll into the shape of a ping-pong.
5. Pour 3 cups of stock in a saucepan. Add in 1 tsp. salt, 2 tbsp. oil. Put rice balls in when stock starts boiling. Cook until rice balls float up. Add in washed green vegetable and bring to boil again. Serve hot.

乾蒸豬肉賣

材料：皮—麵粉２安
　　　　筋粉２安
　　　　蛋２隻
　　　　鹼水數滴
　　　　生粉數茶匙作粉焙

　　　餡—瘦肉８安
　　　　肥肉２安
　　　　蝦肉６安
　　　　冬菇２隻
　　　　甘筍２安

調味：鹽１茶匙　　　　古月粉少許
　　　糖１茶匙　　　　生粉１茶匙
　　　生抽１茶匙　　　水３湯匙

製法：①麵粉、筋粉同篩在桌上，中間
　　　　開穴，雞蛋打勻放在穴中，加
　　　　鹼水拌勻，慢慢撥入四週麵粉
　　　　，搓成軟麵團，將麵團搓成長
　　　　條，再切成小塊。

②瘦肉、肥肉洗淨切成幼粒。
③蝦肉洗淨以毛巾吸乾水份切
　加在豬肉中。
④冬菇浸透蒸熟後切幼粒，甘
　飛水後切幼，將所有幼粒同
　大盆中用手撻之，加入調味
　後撈勻。生粉開水慢慢加入
　撻。
⑤將小塊粉團用木棍開薄成圓
　，用小刀挑肉餡放在皮中，
　手揑起燒賣成窄身之圓柱形
　開口處用刀抹平。
⑥蒸籠塗油，將燒賣放入猛火
　約十分鐘。

Shiu My

INGREDIENTS:

PASTRY—

2 oz. plain flour
2 oz. high protein flour
2 eggs
few drops of alkali water
cornstarch for dusting

FILLING—

8 oz. lean pork
2 oz. fat pork
6 oz. shelled shrimp
2 dried mushrooms
2 oz. bamboo shoot

SEASONINGS:

1 tsp. salt
1 tsp. sugar
1 tsp. light soy
dash of pepper
1 tsp. corn flour
1 tbsp. water

METHOD:

1. Sift plain flour and high protein flour on table, make a hollow in the centre. Put in beaten eggs and alkali water, using the hand to work in flour and knead into a soft dough. Make the dough into a long thin roll. Cut into small pieces.
2. Wash and devein shrimps, dry with a piece of cloth. Dice and put into mixing bowl.
3. Wash and dice lean pork and fat pork. Soak, steam and dice mushrooms. Boil and dice bamboo shoots.
4. Finally put all the ingredients into mixing bowl and pound until firm. Add in seasonings, corn flour and pound again. Mix ingredients well.
5. Roll out pastry into a thin round and put in filling. Dust pastry with cornstarch. Use one hand to hold and shape into a column. Using a knife, flatten the filling on top.
6. Put shiu my in a greased steamer and steam over high heat for 10 minutes.

REMARKS: Bamboo shoots can be substituted by shredded carrot.

Demonstrated by Mrs Pang Fung Ling of Dim Sum Course

山竹蒸牛肉

材料： 牛肉½磅　　　　牙硝¼茶匙
　　　　肥肉1安　　　　熱水2安
　　　　菓皮1小片　　　腐皮1塊
　　　　葱1條

調味： 鹽¾茶匙　　　　古月粉少許
　　　　糖1茶匙　　　　生粉1茶匙
　　　　梳打粉半茶匙　　水2安
　　　　生抽1茶匙　　　生油2安
　　　　蔴醬1茶匙

製法： ①牛肉洗淨抹乾，放入搞肉機中
　　　　　搞爛。
　　　　②肥肉焓熟切成幼粒，菓皮以熱
　　　　　水浸透切成茸，葱亦切成幼粒
　　　　　，放置一旁候用。
　　　　③牙硝用2安熱水浸溶，加入牛
　　　　　肉中，然後加入鹽糖及梳打粉
　　　　　用手撈勻醃半小時。
　　　　④將牛肉轉放深盆中，用手撻之
　　　　　，隨撻隨加生粉水。
　　　　⑤撻至牛肉起膠後加入肥肉粒　，

菓皮茸，葱粒，蔴醬、生抽及
古月粉搓勻，最後逐少加入生
油撻至完全混合爲止。
⑥將牛肉做成小球形。
⑦腐皮抹淨炸透剪開，放在小碟
　中，牛肉球放在腐皮上，將碟
　子放入蒸籠內。
⑧鑊中水煮沸，將蒸籠放入蒸約
　至九分鐘即熟。

Steamed Minced Beef Ball

INGREDIENTS:

½ lb. beef
1 oz. fat pork
a small piece of old tangerine peel
1 green onion
¼ tsp. nitre
2 oz. hot water
1 bean curd sheet

SEASONINGS:

¾ tsp. salt
1 tsp. sugar
½ tsp. soda
1 tsp. sesame paste
1 tsp. light soy
dash of pepper
1 tsp. cornstarch
2 oz. water
2 oz. oil

METHOD:

1. Wash and dry beef, put in meat mincer to mince.
2. Boil and dice fat pork. Soak tangerine peel in warm water until soft, smash. Chop green onion and leave aside.
3. Soak nitre in 2 oz. warm water until dissolved. Add onto beef, together with salt, sugar and soda, mix well and marinade for ½ an hour.
4. Put beef in a mixing bowl and pound well. Dissolve cornstarch in water and pour in solution gradually while pounding the beef.
5. Mix well with diced fat, smashed tangerine peel, green onion, sesame paste, pepper and light soy. Add in oil little at a time and pound until well mixed.
6. Make minced beef into small balls.
7. Wash and dry bean curd sheet, deep fry and cut into small pieces. Put 2 pieces in a small dish with 2 meat balls on top. Place dishes into steamer.
8. Put steamer above boiling water to steam for 8-10 minutes.

REMARKS: Bean curd sheet can be substituted by water cress.

Demonstrated by Tammy Leung of Dim Sum Course.

鬆化椰絲堆

材料： 皮—麵粉10安
　　　　　發粉1½茶匙
　　　　　幼糖2安
　　　　　豬油2安
　　　　　雞蛋1隻
　　　　　清水3湯匙
　　　　餡—鮮椰絲3安
　　　　　糖4安
　　　　　芝蔴一安
　　　　　瓜子肉½安
　　　　　另芝蔴1杯洒面

製法： ①麵粉發粉同篩在桌上開穴，將
　　　　　幼糖、豬油、雞蛋及清水放入
　　　　　穴內以手拌勻，撥入四週之麵
　　　　　粉輕輕搓成一軟團。
　　　　②鮮椰絲放在大盆中，加糖拌勻。
　　　　③芝蔴洗淨置白鑊中文火炒香，
　　　　　與瓜子肉一同加入椰絲糖中，
　　　　　拌勻候用。
　　　　④桌上洒少許粉焙，將粉團取出
　　　　　搓成長條，平均分做二十份至

廿四份。
⑤每份小粉團以手捏成小窩，
　入椰餡，收口搓成圓球形。
⑥芝蔴洗淨隔去水份，放入笪
　中，將圓球滾至沾滿芝蔴。
⑦油一鍋燒至微沸，將椰絲堆
　入，文火炸至金黃色撈起隔
　油。

Deep Fried Sesame Ball

INGREDIENTS:

PASTRY—

10 oz. flour
1½ tsp. baking powder
2 oz. sugar
2 oz. lard
1 egg
3 tbsp. water

FILLING—

3 oz. fresh shredded coconut
4 oz. sugar
1 oz. sesame seeds
½ oz. dried melon seed (shelled)
1 cup sesame seeds for coating

METHOD:

1. Sift flour and baking powder together on table, make a hollow in the centre, put in sugar, lard and beaten egg. Stir together until dissolved. Slowly work in flour, adding in water gradually. Knead into a soft dough.
2. Put shredded coconut into a mixing bowl, add sugar and mix well.
3. Wash sesame seeds, dry and fry over slow fire in a clean wok. Mix well with melon seeds and coconut.
4. Sift a little flour on table, knead soft dough into a long roll, divide into 20 to 24 equal portions.
5. Knead each portion into the shape of a nest, put in filling. Pinch edges together and seal. Roll into a round ball.
6. Wash another 1 cup sesame seeds, drain and pour into bowl. Put balls into bowl and coat with sesame seeds.
7. Heat pan with oil until boiling, lower the fire and put in sesame balls. Deep fry until light brown.

上湯蝦肉餃

材料： 皮—筋粉5安　　餡—蝦肉1磅
　　　　　鷄蛋2隻　　　　　枚肉6安
　　　　　鹼水1茶匙　　　　大地魚2安
　　　　　　　　　　　　　　冬菇1安
　　　　　　　　　　　　　　冬笋2安
　　　　　　　　　　　　　　雞蛋1隻

調味： 鹽$1\frac{1}{2}$茶匙
　　　　糖1茶匙
　　　　古月粉$\frac{1}{2}$茶匙
　　　　蔴油少許
　　　　生粉1茶匙

製法： ①筋粉篩在桌上開穴。將蛋打爛
　　　　　加入與鹼水混和。慢慢撥入麵
　　　　　粉搓成軟麵團。
　　　　②將麵團放在桌上，洒以少許生
　　　　　粉。用木棍輾薄，再掃上生粉
　　　　　，摺起再輾薄。如是摺疊數次
　　　　　，把麵輾至夠薄，切成$2\frac{1}{2}$吋
　　　　　方形。

③冬菇浸透洗淨切碎，蝦肉切
　，枚肉切指甲片，冬笋出水
　切幼，大地魚炸香搗碎，全
　放大盆內加調味品撈勻，用
　略撻，加入雞蛋拌勻。
④餃皮平放桌上，用餐刀撥入
　料約一湯匙，將皮對角摺成
　角，打亂褶少許做成餃形。
⑤爐上置沸水一鍋，將水餃放
　煮五分鐘至浮起，撈起過冷
⑥上湯6杯煮沸，加入水餃滾
　刻，盛在已放菫王生抽及油
　湯窩內，可配時菜數片。

Shrimp Dumplings in Soup

INGREDIENTS:

PASTRY—

5 oz. high protein flour
2 eggs
1 tsp. alkali water

FILLING—

1 lb. shelled shrimps
6 oz. lean pork
2 oz. bamboo shoots
1 oz. mushroom
2 dried plaice
1 egg

SEASONINGS:

1¼ tsp. salt
1 tsp. sugar
¼ tsp. pepper
dash of sesame oil
1 tsp. cornstarch

METHOD:

1. Sieve high protein flour on table and make a hollow in centre. Mix well beaten egg and alkali water in centre. Slowly work in flour and knead into a soft dough.
2. Sieve a little cornstarch on table. Roll soft dough into thin pastry, seive a little starch on top, fold and roll out until very thin. Repeat several times, finally cut into 2½ in. squares.
3. Soak, wash and chop mushroom, dice shrimps, and lean pork. Boil and dice bamboo shoots, deep fry and mince plaice. Place all ingredients into mixing bowl and mix well. Pound and stir in beaten egg.
4. Place pastry flat on table. Use knife to place in 1 tbsp. filling, fold in a triangle with plaits along the edge.
5. Boil a pan of water over oven, put in dumplings to boil for 5 minutes until floated. Drain and place into a bowl of cold water.
6. Boil 6 cups stock, add in dumpling to cook for a while, place in bowl together with stock, leek, light soy and oil. A few pieces of green vegetables can be added.

GENERAL TERMS IN DIM SUM

1. **BAKE:**
   To cook in oven by dry heat.

2. **BAKE BLIND:**
   Line pie shell with grease proof paper & half-fill with rice or beans. Bake in hot oven till pastry is nearly cooked. Remove beans & paper then return to oven to complete baking.

3. **BIND:**
   To add liquid or egg to a mixture to hold it together.

4. **BLEND:**
   To mix ingredients to a smooth paste.

5. **BRUSH:**
   To put beaten egg or sugar solution on top of pastry to give a glossy appearance.

6. **CHOP:**
   To cut nuts into tiny pieces.

7. **COAT:**
   To cover food with flour or to brush with egg & coat with crumps or batter.

8. **CREAM:**
   To mix ingredients, often fat & sugar, to the consistancy of cream.

9. **DRAW IN:**
   To fold flour into ingredients to mix together.

10. **DECORATE:**
    To furnish with ornamental ingredients.

11. **DICE:**
    To cut into even cubes.

12. **FOLD:**
    To flick ingredients gently together.

13. **KNEAD:**
    To pull & stretch the dough in order to develop the gluten strength & so ensure an even texture & good volume.

14. **PINCH:**
To draw edges together & seal.

15. **POUND:**
To beat against table in order to make it elastic & firm.

16. **PROVE:**
To allow dough to rise.

17. **RUB – IN:**
To incorporate fat & flour together.

18. **SCALD:**
To heat milk almost to boiling point.

19. **SIFT:**
To shake dry ingredients through a sieve to remove any lumps.

20. **STIR:**
To beat up in circles to mix evenly.

21. **WHISK:**
To beat briskly to thicken cream or egg white.

22. **WORK IN:**
To fold flour into centre to mix with other ingredients.

23. **WRAP:**
To fold up pastry to hold filling.

點心常用術語解釋

1. **烘**—— 不用油而放入焗爐中焗至乾硬
2. **塗油**—— 搽上油或流質於食物上使其不致乾燥，尤其適用於炙肉時。
3. **混合**—— 將固體或流質之材料混在一起。
4. **塗蛋**—— 將打匀之蛋黃液體塗在批皮上使其光澤。
5. **切碎**—— 將食物剁成小塊。
6. **裹**—— 把食物滾上一層麵粉、麵包糠、粉漿或蛋液。
7. **打軟**—— 將材料混合，（多數以油、糖為主）搞拌成奶油狀。
8. **製飾**—— 將蛋羔或餅加彩色裝飾物點綴之。
9. **切細**—— 切成均等骰子狀。
10. **覆入**—— 慢慢捲入拌匀。
11. **搓**—— 反覆按匀粉團，令粉中麵筋發揮作用，和成一塊軟滑粉團。
12. **捏**—— 將粉團邊沿向入捏成花紋。
13. **發**—— 使粉團發起。
14. **擦入**—— 將硬牛油放入麵粉中擦成碎屑。
15. **篩**—— 除去塊狀麵粉及雜質。
16. **蒸**—— 放於蒸籠內隔水用猛火蒸燉。
17. **攪拌**—— 以順時鐘或反時鐘方向搞動和匀。
18. **打起**—— 以快速手法打蛋白或忌廉使其濃厚。
19. **撥**—— 將麵粉撥入中央。
20. **包起**—— 以窩形盛載餡料，然後封口。
21. **撻**—— 將麵糰用力拋擲在桌上，使其乾身及軟韌

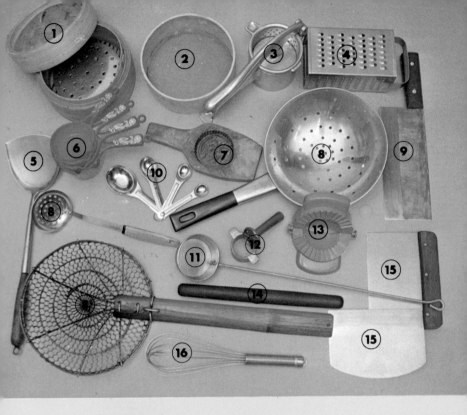

Cooking Utensils

1.	Steamer	蒸籠
2.	Sieve	篩
3.	Juicer	搾汁器
4.	Grater	羌磨
5.	Turning spade	鑊鏟
6.	Measuring cups	量杯
7.	Wooden cake mould	木餅印
8.	Strainers	笊籬
9.	Pastry knife	拍皮刀
10.	Measuring spoons	量匙
11.	Deep fry cake mould	油提
12.	Soft cake mould	軟餅印
13.	Revioli mould	餃子模
14.	Chinese rolling-pin	麵棍
15.	Scraping knives	刮刀
16.	Egg beater	打蛋器

辨五穀・釋疑難

　　五穀之中，米及玉蜀黍多生於熱帶地區，爲東方人之主要食糧。小麥、大麥及粿麥則產於溫帶，爲西方人所重用，以下是五穀之分析及用途介紹：

1 米：以米作食糧之人口幾佔地球之半，產於中國、印度、日本、暹羅等地，用途廣闊，種類亦多，主要分爲二大類：

　　A 粘米——燒飯、煮粥、釀酒等。

　　粘米粉——蒸糕、煎咸薄餅、製造發粉。

　　炒米粉——軟、硬炒米餅。

　　B 糯米——包粽、有味飯、甜粥等。

　　糯米粉——年糕、湯團、軟糍。

　　熟糯粉（即糕粉）——餅餡、香蕉糕。

2 小麥：以小麥作食糧之人口亦佔地球之半，最普遍用途爲製造麵包、麵條。主要分二大類：

　　A 硬麥——多產於乾燥陽光充足之地如加拿大。含大量蛋白質，使人精力充沛。麥粒堅硬，蛋白質含量約十至十五％。韌性強、含有大量麵筋原料——麩素。磨粉後即爲筋粉。粉中之筋與水混和後轉韌，使麵團有彈性。放焗爐加熱後則膨脹，以致成爲鬆軟之麵飽。

　　1 高筋粉——蛋白含量爲十二至十五％。宜做通心粉、意粉、油條、麵包、擘酥等。

　　2 中筋粉——蛋白含量約十至十二％。宜做酥餅雲吞皮之類。

　　3 汀麵——將筋粉放於布袋中，置水盆內揉之。揉出之粉質沉於水中，晒乾後即爲汀麵。宜做蝦餃 粉果等。袋中黏性麵團則爲麵筋。

　　B 軟麵——產於較陰暗潮濕地區如西歐、英國、美國東部等地。麵粒剖開後呈粉狀。蛋白含量約七至十％，韌性較弱，磨粉後即成普通麵粉。

　　1 普通麵粉——餅乾、乾果蛋糕、批皮、曲奇、克力架、冬栗等。（糕餅甜品書中將有詳述。）

　　2 自發粉——普通麵粉一磅加梳打粉⅓安加他他粉⅔安混合篩勻即可。宜做簡便蛋糕、脆漿等。

3 大麥：最能適應環境，能生長於貧脊之土壤中。

　　A 整粒——多用於製麥芽以供：

　　1 釀酒

　　2 製麥芽糖

　　B 加工後成爲洋薏米——宜煮湯及作紅燒肉之配料，與檸檬混和製成菓汁。

4 粿麥： 以爲一種旣黑且硬之穀粒，味帶酸。產於較冷地帶及劣
土中。鈣質比其他穀類較高，爲歐陸中層社會人仕之主
要食糧，粿麥粉之麵筋含量極少，故難獨當一面製造麵
包，多與小麥粉同用。

　　A 粿麥粉──製造黑麵包及一種薄餅乾。

　　B 製造威士忌、氈酒、伏特加等。

5 玉蜀黍： （又名粟米）產於較熱地方如美國、意大利等國家之
南部。

　　A 整個放於水中、加糖焓熟，塗牛油而食。

　　B 將粟米粒削出，與其他什菜粒肉丁混合炒熟做菜。

　　C 粟米可搾油及製粟膠。

　　D 粟米粉及吉士粉──做布甸、糕餅、有凝結作用。

　　E 漿粉──漿硬衣服、床單等、並可製漿糊。

CEREALS and FLOUR

Among all the cereals, rice and maize are grown in tropical area, they are the main food for the Eastern population. While wheat, barley and rye are grown in temperate region and are more important to the people in Europe.

1. **RICE** — The main food for about half of all the people in the world, grown in China, India, Japan, and Siam. There are thousands of kinds of rice being used in various way. Rice is divided into 2 main streams :—

A. Rice (whole grain) — Used as cooked rice, congee, fermented beer.
   when ground to powder — rice flour : Pudding
                                         thin cakes
                                         baking powder
              cooked rice flour : hard and soft cakes

B. Glutinous rice (whole grain) — Dumpling, tasty rice, sweet congee.
   when ground into powder — Glutinous rice flour : New Year-
                                                      Pudding
                                                      rice balls
                                                      soft cakes
                 cooked glutinous flour : cake filling
                                           banana fin-
                                           gers

2. **WHEAT** — The grain most widely used by ½ of the population in the world, usually used in making bread and noodles. Divided into 2 main streams :—

A. Hard wheat — Grown in the driest, suniest areas such as Canada, contains 10-15% protein which gives us strength. Strong and flinty when cut across. When ground to powder it forms high protein flour, after mixing with water makes yeast dough elastic. When put in oven and bake, dough rises and form bread.
   i. High protein flour — contain 12 — 15% protein.
                            Spaghetti macaroni, bread, crisp
                            and deep fry cruller etc.

ii. Low protein flour — contain 10 — 12% protein, used in making crisp and won ton pastry etc.

iii. Wheat starch — Put protein flour into cotton bag, place in basin of water and knead until powder leaks. out. When remaining water evaporated, the sediment forms wheat starch.
Wheat starch is suitable for making shrimp dumpling and ravioli. The sticky flour dough inside the bag is gluten.

B. Soft wheat — Grown in duller, wetter climate such as Western Europe and Eastern United States. The grain looks floury when cut across. Contains 7-10% protein. Less elastic. When ground to powder forms plain flour.

i. Plain flour — Biscuits, short crust pastry, cookies, crackers, fruit cakes etc.

ii. Self raising flour — (1 lb. plain flour + ¼ oz. bicarbonate soda + 3/8 oz. cream of tartar mix together) suitable for baking plain cakes, crisp batter etc.

3. **BARLEY** — Can be grown in poor soil.

A. Barley grains are usually used after malted, to make beer or malt.
B. Kernel of barley are made into pearl barley for soups and pudding by being stripped of their sheath and polished. Drinks made by boiling pearl barley are very good for health.

4. **RYE** — A kind of dark and hard cereal grain, grown in colder climate. Rye contains more calcium than any other cereal and tastes sour. It is a cereal which is more important to the people in the continent of Europe. Rye flour contains less gluten, which holds the bread together in elastic masses, so it should be used together with wheat flour. It is also used in making whisky, gin and vodka.

5. **MAIZE** — Grown in tropical areas such as South America and South Italy.

    i. Can be boiled to eat.

   ii. Grain — Whole kernel is used in hot dishes.
              Grind into creamy style to make soup.

  iii. To make oil. Corn oil for cooking, corn syrup for cakes.
      When ground to powder — 1. Corn starch, custard powder for baking cakes and pudding, has the ability to solidify.
                                     2. Starch for stiffening clothes, and glue for envelopes.

Weight And Measure

Britain and Canada	America and Australia
1 lb. butter or other fat	2 cups
1 lb. flour	4 cups
1 lb. granulated sugar	2¼ cups
1 lb. chopped or minced meat (firmly packed)	2 cups
½ oz. flour	2 tablespoons
1 oz. sugar	2 tablespoons
1 oz. butter	2 tablespoons

Metric Equivalents

Imperial		Metric
1 oz.	=	28 grs.
4 oz.	=	112 grs.
½ lb. (8 oz.)	=	225 grs.
1 lb. (16 oz.)	=	453 grs.
2.2 lb.	=	1 kilo

Cup Measures

8 fluid oz. = 1 American cup = ½ pint

Spoon Measures

1/6 fluid oz.	=	1 American teaspoon
½ fluid oz.	=	1 American tablespoon
1 tablespoon	=	3 teaspoons = 20 ml.

Liquid Measures

4 fluid oz. = 1 gill	= ½ cup	= 5/6 Imperial gill = 125 ml.
16 fluid oz. = 1 pint	= 2 cups	= 5/6 Imperial pint = 500 ml.
1 quart = 2 pints	= 5/6 Imperial quart	
1 gallon = 4 quarts	= 5/6 Imperial gal.	
1 litre = 4½ cups	= 35 fluid oz.	

Oven Temperature

Description of Oven	Approx. Temperature Centre of Oven		Thermostat Setting	
Very low or	200-250 F°	100-130 C°	¼ = 225 F°	107 C°
Very cool	250-300	130-150	½ = 250	121
			1 = 290	143
Very moderate	300-350	150-180	2 = 310	154
			3 = 335	168
Moderate	350-375	180-190	4 = 350	177
Moderately hot or			5 = 375	191
Hot	375-400	190-210	6 = 400	204
Hot to very hot	425-450	220-225	7 = 425	218
Very hot	450-500	230-260	8 = 450	232
			9 = 470	243

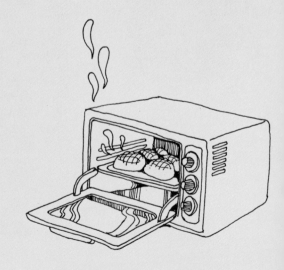

美點佳餚書集介紹

美點佳餚 1 HK $12.00

綜合食譜

內容包括：小菜・快餐・海鮮・湯羹・燒鹵・
全鷄・東南亞菜・點心・西餐・
糕餅甜品。

內容充實＊彩色鮮艷＊解釋詳盡＊印刷精美

CHOPSTICKS RECIPES 1 INTRODUCTION

AN EASY GUIDE TO CHINESE COOKERY.
A PERFECT GIFT TO BE KEPT IN MEMORY.
A DIRECT REFERENCE FOR D.S. STUDENTS.
A MUST FOR GOURMETS' COLLECTIONS.

美點佳餚 3 HK $12.00

吉祥菜譜

內容包括：鷄・鴨・鴿・猪・羊・魚・蝦・
蟹・翅・什項等製法・

過年時節＊語貴吉祥＊嘉饌名餚＊美味芬香

CHOPSTICKS RECIPES 3 TRADITIONAL DISHES

Best hot dishes during Chinese New Year,
Traditional customs understood right and clear

美點佳餚4　HK$12.00
省時快餐

內容包括：各式粉・麵・飯之快速調製法

廚務繁忙＊生活緊張＊快餐省時＊更富營養

CHOPSTICKS RECIPES 4
QUICK MEALS

Save time! Save money!
Why not make everybody happy?

美點佳餚5　HK$12.00
每日菜譜

內容包括：家常午餐晚餐
　　　　　各項菜式52款

每日菜譜＊耳熟能詳＊圖文並茂＊款款優良

CHOPSTICKS RECIPES 5
EVERYDAY MENU

Everyday Menu contains exhaustive range of daily
and festive recipes based on the lectures in
Commercial Radio given by the author.

美點佳餚6　HK$12.00
西餅麵包

內容包括：各式蛋糕・西餅・撻・批・
布甸・麵包之詳細製法・

早餐茶點＊西餅麵包＊東方色彩＊包羅萬有

CHOPSTICKS RECIPES 6
CAKES AND BREAD

Cakes & Bread for breakfast and for tea
Recipes of oriental style for you and me

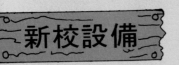

新校設備

中菜室

CHINESE DISHES SECTION

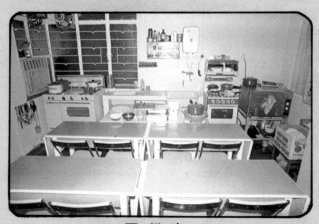

西餅室

CAKE AND BREAD SECTION

WEDDING CAKE COURSE

1. 印尼學生實習結婚餅

   Indonesian students practicing wedding Cake.

2. 印尼學員在兩週內完成婚餅及花餅速成班

   Mrs. Wibowo Susilo & Frieda Herawasi from Indonesia graduated in Cake Decoration Course.

3. 印尼棉蘭之謝玉蘭女士作婚餅實習

   Madam Lanny Ke Surln from Indonesia practicing her Wedding Cake.

OVERSEAS
MAIL ORDER FORM

We accept mail order from all over the world except in countries where we have already had a sole agent.

Chopsticks Recipes

_____ copies Book 1 — Introduction @ HK$12.00 each	= HK$_____
_____ copies Book 2 — Dim Sum @ HK12.00 each	= HK$_____
_____ copies Book 3 — Traditional Dishes @HK$12.00 each	= HK$_____
_____ copies Book 4 — Quick Meals @HK$12.00 each	= HK$_____
_____ copies Book 5 — Everyday Menu @HK$12.00 each	= HK$_____
_____ copies Book 6 — Cakes and Bread @HK$12.00 each	= HK$_____
Registered P. and P. for _____ copies	= HK$_____
Total	= HK$_____

I enclose a bank draft/cheque to the value of HK$ _____ crossed and made payable to Chopsticks Cooking Centre.

Name: _____

Address: _____

_____

Please send to: Mail Order Department
Chopsticks Cooking Centre
Kowloon Central P.O. Box 3515
HONG KONG

Registered Postage and Packing for

1 copy	HK$ 5.00
2 copies	HK$ 6.00
3 copies	HK$ 8.00
4 copies	HK$ 9.00
5 copies	HK$10.00
6 copies	HK$10.00
10 copies	HK$12.00
20 copies	HK$20.00

Special discount for Retailer and Sole Distributor

點心班
Dim Sum Course

點心夜班學員在分享製成品

A. Students of Dim sum Class tasting the Cha Shiu Buns they made by themselves.

印尼,星加坡及馬來西亞學員實習叉燒飽及豆沙飽

B. Students from Indonesia, Singapore & Malaysia practicing Cha Shiu Bun & Sweet paste Bun.

外地學員實習猪腸粉

C. Oversea Students practicing Ricesheet Roll (Chu Cheung Fun).

烹飪科
DIFFERENT COOKERY COURSES

Vegetarian Dishes Course	延年素菜班
Chinese Dishes Course	正宗粵菜班
Chinese Roasts Course	各類燒烤班
Dim Sum Course	初高點心班
Western Dishes Course	酒店西餐班
Vegetable Carving Course	蔬菓雕花班
Professional Bread Course	職業麵飽班
Cake & Pastry Course	高級西餅班
Wedding Cake Course	結婚禮餅班
Moon Cake Course	全科月餅班
Deep Fried Pastry Course	各式油器班
Beancurd Course	馳名豆腐班
Noodle Course	打麵全科班
Ice & Butter Sculpture	冰雕牛油班
2-Week Ordinary Intensive Course	2 週特選速成班
2-Week Professional Intensive Course	2 週職業速成班
8-Week Ordinary Cookery Course	8 週全科烹飪班
12-Week Professional Cookery Course	12週職業廚師班
1-3 Day Individual Tourist Course	1-3天個別遊客班
1-3 Day Tourist Group Course	1-3天集體遊客班

其他各科
OTHER SUBJECTS

Fashion Design Course	時裝繪描班
Pattern Drafting Course	女服紙樣班
Knitting & Crochet Course	編織鈎織班
Floral Course	草月流插花班
Professional Beautician Course	職業美容師班
Professional Hair Style Course	職業美髮師班
Professional Acupuncture Course	職業指壓按穴班
Flower Design Course	絲帶絲絨花班
Photography Course	攝影速成班
Crocheted Puppies Course	鈎織寵物班